# A JANE AUSTEN QUINTET

By the same author

*Shakespeare's God*, a study of the four great tragedies

*Jane Austen & the Interplay of Character*

*Hamlet, King of Denmark*, a new tragicomical ending

# A Jane Austen Quintet

Critical Inquiries into the Novels' World

**IVOR MORRIS**

Some of these studies previously appeared
in issues of *Persuasions*, journal of the
Jane Austen Society of North America

Printed and published by Sarsen Press
22 Hyde Street, Winchester SO23 7DR

Copyright © Ivor Morris 2008

Ivor Morris is hereby identified as author of this work in accordance with the Copyright, Designs and Patents Act of 1988. All rights are reserved. Apart from any fair dealing for the purpose of private study, research, criticism or review, as permitted under the Copyright Act, 1956, no part of this publication may be reproduced, stored in a retrieval system, or transmitted, in any form or by any means, electronic, electrical, chemical, mechanical, optical, photocopying, recording or otherwise, without the prior permission in writing of the copyright owner.

British Library Cataloguing-in-Publication Data
A CIP catalogue record for this book is available
from the British Library

ISBN 978-0-9558387-0-5

To

S. P. E.

# Contents

| | |
|---|---|
| Preface | ix |
| Jane Austen and Her Men | 1 |
| *Persuasion*'s Unwritten Story | 37 |
| Elizabeth and Mr. Bennet | 73 |
| The Enigma of Harriet Smith | 96 |
| The Prisoner of Mansfield Park | 121 |
| Notes | 147 |

Along with her comedy sense she possessed a subtle insight into the moral nature of man. The union of the two is the distinguishing characteristic of her achievement; and it makes these lively unpretentious comedies of social and domestic life the vehicle of profound and illuminating comments on the human drama.

Lord David Cecil, *A Portrait of Jane Austen*, 1978.

# Preface

The topics discussed in the following pages arise directly from interpretation of Jane Austen's novels. They are considered with a thoroughness such matters do not always command in criticism, as befits the investigative intent the studies have in common. Their predominant concern is with personality, mainly but by no means exclusively that of the heroine; and the context of outlook and assumption in which characters act and are acted upon is closely observed throughout.

The bracketed numbers accompanying quotations relate to the pages of R. W. Chapman's standard Oxford edition (1932 – ) of the novels, and will enable readers easily to consult the text upon issues under review.

To a present-day understanding, personality is a unique possession, a "given" of a man or woman's identity. But for Jane Austen it was not a matter of fixed distinctiveness. She and the readership she addressed tended to regard persons as conditioned and moulded by the society they were part of: its conventions, norms and pressures. As they journeyed through life, therefore, theirs was not so much a state of being as of becoming: one of consistently attaining to selfhood rather than simply possessing it. To such a perception, man in fact was less an entity in himself than a social phenomenon, partly at least drawing distinctiveness from his dealings with those around him.

That this idea of individuality belonged to an age which has vanished does not mean that it was mistaken. Could it, indeed, be closer to the truth than the view most of us hold today? And might it be to a real extent responsible for the freshness, modernity, and enduring appeal of the world and the people Jane Austen sets before us?

It is a pleasure to record my indebtedness to friend and assistant Ceri Thomson, herself a Jane Austen devotee of wide literary interests, for her accomplished presentation of the manuscript and encouragement in this undertaking.

Ivor Morris

# i

# Jane Austen and Her Men

"Faults are in flesh", laments the bard, "as motes be in the sun". Jane Austen's distinction lies in her showing that this need not be a cry of despair. She presents us with the auspicious paradox of a sharp-eyed realist relentlessly critical of humankind, yet benignly compassionate towards it – and able, what is more, to convert the instincts of the reader to her own charitable regard. All who have experience of that conversion must wonder at it; and even where it might not be present, a book of hers will rarely be set aside without the thought, "That strain I heard was of a higher mood"[1]. Consciousness that she is dealing with, and reconciling us to, a flawed humanity is at once part of the secret of her dedication and a source of the enduring interest and appeal of her portrayal of men and women. And if her Mr. Knightley can find his domestic bliss in an Emma who is "faultless in spite of all her faults", we may be in no doubt that Mrs. Knightley will in due time find cause enough to come to a corresponding appreciation of the man who is now her life's companion.

The subject of Jane Austen's men brings to memory a shrewd elderly widow of my early acquaintance, who on occasion would give me the benefit of her wisdom. Once, the topic of matrimony having arisen, she confided, "It's dead easy for a woman to keep a man". "Is that so?" I inquired politely. "Simple", was the rejoinder. "Just flatter them. Make them think they're wonderful". I was mildly affronted at an estimate of my sex that made them out to be helpless victims of the vanity and pride Mary Bennet had so platitudinously pronounced human nature to be prone to. But I must confess to having pondered the matter since then.

Jane Austen does, to be sure, give us examples of vanity rampant in men. One need only consider Sir William Lucas, who, having upon being knighted developed a distaste for residence in a small country town, removed from Meryton to Lucas Lodge, "where he could think with pleasure of his own importance"; or a person more grandly addicted, of whose character we are told, "Vanity was the beginning and the end". The handsomeness and the baronetcy which he enjoyed were for him the highest of blessings: "and the Sir Walter Elliot, who united these gifts, was the constant object of his warmest respect and devotion". The same may be concluded of Mr. Collins, who not only cannot conceive that any woman should reject him as suitor, but regards the office of parson "as equal in point of dignity with the highest rank in the kingdom".

These lesser characters embodying an extreme of vanity put one in mind of Shakespeare's Dogberry who, on being named an ass by his betters, protests with felicitous fury,

> I am a wise fellow, and, which is more, an officer, and, which is more, a householder, and, which is more, as pretty a piece of flesh as any is in Messina, and one that knows the law, go to; and a rich fellow enough, go to; and a fellow that hath had losses, and one that hath two gowns and everything handsome about him[2].

When it comes to the vanity or pride of possession, he speaks for many greater than himself who are to be found in Jane Austen's novels. General Tilney, certainly, derives no small satisfaction from the vast Abbey he is master of, and the magnificence of its dining room, "of which… the General could not forego the pleasure of pacing out the length, for the more certain information" of the unconcerned Catherine Morland. But can we for a moment doubt that, in quieter ways, pride of ownership also suffuses Mr. Darcy, Sir Thomas Bertram and Mr. Rushworth, the possessors of Pemberley, Mansfield Park and Sotherton Court? And the prospective possessors, too – like Miss Eliza Bennet, who upon her first setting eyes on it, "felt, that to be mistress of Pemberley might be something!" or Emma Woodhouse, whom "the respectable size and style" of Mr. Knightley's Donwell Abbey, her destined home, moves to an "honest pride and complacency", no less; or Maria Bertram, whose "Rushworth-feelings" become so obviously pronounced in the vicinity of Sotherton, and whose spirits, as the barouche drives up to its principal entrance, are " in as happy a flutter as vanity and pride could furnish"?

From pride and vanity in this and other forms few can be free; and the comedian's task is to set the snares of ridicule for it in the social context, and laugh us back to sense. But it is a long step from a Dogberry to a Malvolio or a Shylock – to personalities in whom self-regard has become obsessive, and a controlling force. Neither the entreaties of good-nature nor the techniques of the happy ending can assuage the hurt they suffer: comedy fades, and drama takes on tragic tones as they leave the stage unappeased, vowing or dreaming of revenge. They draw us with them away from the fragile fabric of man's society to the sheer cliff face of things: for tragedy's role is to display the essence of our human nature to us. Its protagonist heroes we can identify with, for, though built on a bigger scale, they are entirely like ourselves. And their motivation can be summed up in a single word: pride.

Othello goes forward with an absolute belief in himself – in what he consciously terms, "My parts, my title, and my perfect soul"[3]. Lear's self-concept is an innate royalty of disposition: in his madness he professes himself, significantly, "Ay, every inch a king: / When I do stare, see how the subject quakes"[4]. Disaster for him comes through a refusal to be treated as anything less than his own estimate of himself. Macbeth murders his way to the "golden round" because it will, as he assumes, confer a deserved greatness upon him. Hamlet alone abandons the path of pride. Though he can find it in himself, like the others, to "do such bitter business as the day / Would quake to look on"[5] in propitiation of his own image, he turns from the tragic self-assertion to become, in Dr. Johnson's words, "an instrument rather than an agent"[6] – acted upon, rather than himself acting.

It is a woman, in the person of Lady Macbeth, who makes plain what lies at the heart of the heroic pretence. Her husband hesitates at his appalling task: it is for her to steel him to resolution. She does so by appealing to the basic quality of manhood within him – and succeeds by taunting him with the lack of it:

> Art thou afeard
> To be the same in thine own act and valour
> As thou art in desire?[7]

Are you afraid to assert what you have it in you to do, and to be? In that scornful challenge is revealed that it is pride in himself which makes her man, and any man, what he is: that self-esteem is the dominant constituent of the male ego: that, in truth, men most characteristically need to have the feeling that they are wonderful!

Why, in discussing Jane Austen's men, do I argue from Shakespeare? Because he was her tutor. As she says in Henry Crawford, speaking for herself, "Shakespeare one gets acquainted with without knowing how. It is a part of an Englishman's constitution…… one is intimate with him by instinct". And, as a fellow dramatist, though writing in novel form – Macaulay is not alone in rating her second only to him[8] – she likewise will fathom the soul of man, as of woman. Do, then, her heroes also exhibit the heroic pride? For an answer, I would point to what is less than half a hero – to the young Lucas who happens to overhear Elizabeth and Mrs. Bennet in agreement upon the detestable pride of the rich Mr. Darcy, and Mary's ensuing observations upon that failing. "If I were as rich as Mr. Darcy", he pipes up, "I should not care how proud I was. I would keep a pack of foxhounds, and drink a bottle of wine every day". And when Mrs. Bennet interposes that he would be drinking a good deal more than he ought, and that if she were to see him at it she would take away his bottle directly, " The boy protested that she should not; she continued to declare that she would, and the argument ended only with the visit". This young gentleman will patently not be afeard to be the same in his own act and valour as he is in desire. The child here is father of the man, is he not? More than that: he is the very archetype.

Is he, though? Surely this exalted notion of the self is not evident in Jane Austen's men. She is appraising, not man in the abstract, but in the drawing room and dining room: not the bedrock condition, but that fashioned by education, culture, social modes and pressures: personages of the leisure reading of a polite age. Tragic heroes may indeed pursue their own shadow, take a lofty self-regard to its logical conclusion, and go down to splendid or gory destruction; but they are not her concern, her heroes do not imitate them. Indeed, the men of her novels would consciously reject any such grandiose pretension and vaingloriousness as absurd, scorn it as being in the worst possible taste.

Consciously, they would; but what about their more inward promptings? Might it not be that their literary creator is better aware than they of what lurks beneath the urbane surface of their demeanour? Would she not have known, as all do, that her men, like all men, are grown-up schoolboys – and found the demon of their spirits, in almost every case, to be that proud and aspiring Lucas imp? Certain it is that she entertained no sanguine expectation of the youthful male. When the school term ended, and "a countless number of Postchaises full of Boys" from Winchester passed by the cottage at Chawton, she saw them "full of future Heroes, Legislators, Fools, & Vilains"[9]. Can it be that she saw her fictional heroes as exemplars of the vice of pride? Of whom else should we inquire, for a beginning, than the mature Fitzwilliam Darcy?

*   *   *

There is not the least bit of vanity in Mr. Darcy. Why should there be, when he has no need of it – when his rank and his income render him indifferent to what others may think of him? But pride – well-regulated pride – he will admit to: proudly. Not so as to claim to be altogether free of faults: "Perhaps", he concedes accommodatingly to Elizabeth, "that is not possible for any one". But, he assures her, he has made it the study of his life to avoid the more contemptible kinds of weakness. How far short is Darcy here of asserting, with Othello,

"My parts, my title, and my perfect soul"? Not much. Especially when you bear in mind the associated characteristic of an unyielding temper which he so readily confesses: "My good opinion once lost", he affirms, "is lost for ever". For what is Othello's reaction when he loses his good opinion of his friend and comrade, Cassio? It is,

> Cassio, I love thee;
> But never more be officer of mine.[10]

In the earlier Darcy, at least, the heroic pride is strongly evident. There is not only an implicit self-admiration in his attitudes, but a striving after éclat in his speech which Elizabeth has noticed, and had good cause to: a use of scathing unreserve against foe and friend which can impartially charge Bingley with the indirect boast in relation to his handwriting, accuse young ladies of walking about for the purpose of showing off their figures – and remark, concerning his future bride, "*She* a beauty! – I should as soon call her mother a wit". His behaviour at the Netherfield ball proclaims the man. "He walked here, and he walked there, fancying himself so very great!" declares Mrs. Bennet in reporting it. She speaks, as Margaret Kennedy comments, with unusual accuracy[11]. Here struts the pride which goes before a fall.

It is in a woman of course that he meets his Waterloo. Not Caroline Bingley – though with commendable feminine discernment she has offered what would have been the right treatment for a more ordinary mortal, in those flattering compliments upon the speed, the evenness, the delightfulness of his writing, as she watches the progress of his letter to his sister; and upon his possessing, furthermore, qualities of mind and disposition so beyond any reproof as to enable him, were he so disposed, to "hug himself". The difficulty for Caroline is that Darcy is convinced of his being admirable to the point of needing no telling, and has met so many girls who try this tactic as to be heartily weary of it. When, though, he encounters one who will attempt no such thing, but will rather tell him in words as explicit as his own precisely what she thinks of him – who dispels the enrapturing notion of his own consequence – he's lost: goes down like a ninepin.

From a Darcy to a Knightley is a far cry. Here is no pretentious spirit, but "a sensible man about seven or eight and thirty", as plain-dealing and principled as they come. But the question does arise in the novel – in relation to his status, moreover – and it is his own Emma who sees through him. Knightley is a countryman, given to walking round his estate – and to social functions, in disregard of the dignity requisite in that era for persons of any consideration in the world. To the Coles' dinner party, however, he does drive up in a carriage. Emma Woodhouse, following in her own, is pleased; and as he hands her out, observes, "This is coming as you should do, … like a gentleman". Knightley senses and meets the challenge instantly. A carriage, he insists, is irrelevant to the issue: "if we had met first in the drawing room", he tells her, "I doubt whether you would have discerned me to be more of a gentleman than usual". "Yes, I should", she replies – seizing upon an effect Jane Austen herself had often noted in such circumstances. "There is always a look of consciousness or bustle when people come in a way which they know to be beneath them. You think you carry it off very well, I dare say, but with you it is a sort of bravado, an air of affected unconcern..... *Now* you have nothing to try for. You are not afraid of being supposed ashamed. You are not striving to look taller than any body else. *Now* I shall really be very happy to walk into the same room with you".

She has caught him out, in a minor yet pompous affectation. What reply can he make? He doesn't hate her; and he has grace enough to be amused at his own discomfiture. So he just says, "Nonsensical girl!" as must any man when a woman has had the better of the argument. He had presupposed that arriving in a plebeian way could not affect him personally – rather in the manner of Julius Caesar, who, alluding to any menace that might lie in Cassius's disapproval of him, avers to Mark Anthony,

> I rather tell thee what is to be fear'd
> Than what I fear; for always I am Caesar.[12]

So Knightley – though not any kind of tragic hero – had been telling himself, "Whatever style I choose to arrive in, I fear no loss of dignity in my own or others' eyes: for always I am Knightley". He may be replete with estimable qualities, but amongst them pride has some habitation.

But can it inhabit a person in whom we consistently find (to use the author's own words) "the gentleness of an excellent nature"? The fact that Edmund Bertram is a man of the cloth is no indication one way or the other: Jane Austen had been in the company of far too many clergymen to be under illusion that the cleric is from that cause "a thing ensky'd and sainted"[13]. More to the point for her is that Edmund is inescapably his father's son. There is an evident likeness: a mutual trust and understanding exists between them, and both are reflective, moralizing natures. Nothing in fact could have exceeded Sir Thomas's concern that instruction in moral and religious principles should form part of his children's education; but the novel demonstrates how warped his judgment and personal morality can be by the dictates of social consequence. Seeing full well that Maria has neither love nor respect for James Rushworth, he is nevertheless happy to consent to a marriage "which would bring him such an addition of respectability and influence, and very happy to think any thing of his daughter's disposition that was most favourable for the purpose". The same consideration determines his attitude to Fanny Price before she is even in the house. At all costs her being nurtured amongst them must not bring social degradation: Sir Thomas's main object is "to preserve in the minds of my *daughters* the consciousness of what they are". – How acute is Margaret Kennedy's remark that, though he believes he is bringing up his daughters to serve God, "he is really more bent upon fitting them to serve Mansfield Park".

His son she finds to be "in search of some better repository of the good"[14]. He is indeed. But Edmund's quest for it can be bedevilled, believe it or not, by this very consciousness, in his father's terms, of "what he is". Consider the problem that faces him when, through his declining to act in *Lover's Vows*, it is proposed that that most gentlemanly commoner Charles Maddox be invited to make good the deficiency.

Edmund is alarmed at the prospect. He has pained awareness

> "of the mischief that *may*, of the unpleasantness that *must*, arise from a young man's being received in this manner – domesticated among us – authorized to come at all hours – and placed suddenly upon a footing which must do away all restraints".

Every rehearsal in such a situation would tend to create what he terms "licence". The magnanimity with which he admits to knowing no harm of Charles Maddox will not extend to toleration of this "excessive intimacy" and its dread outcome, "familiarity". "I cannot think of it with any patience", he cries – "and it does appear to me an evil of such magnitude as must, *if possible,* be prevented".

Edmund's concept of evil would not withstand theological scrutiny; but in the social context it has an inflexible logic. These are the accents of pride: here speaks the arrogance of rank. In the disdainful idiom of Shakespeare's Prince of Arragon, Edmund has reacted as he does

> Because I will not jump with common spirits
> And rank me with the barbarous multitude.[15]

This imperative obliges him to withdraw his objection over *Lovers' Vows* and take the part of Anhalt against his judgment: a decision which materially affects the progress of events. Fanny sees, and grieves over, her beloved's lapse. And Jane Austen is sympathetically aware of the absurdity in itself of that ingrained presumption in Edmund which has helped to make him what he is. Her confidence and ours rests in the small likelihood of anything similar arising, in the sphere in which he and Fanny will afterwards move, to discompose the graciousness of that excellent nature.

Would Henry Tilney have found as much to unnerve and offend him in a commoner's proximity? In so humoursome, as well as charming a man, we might be inclined to expect a reaction of more amused sort. For Tilney is genuinely witty. Now if wit can be supposed a fault, is it possible, in Hamlet's phrase, for a person to "take corruption" from it?[16] Tilney can be viewed as having succumbed, to the point of turning into a dedicated satirist. Who has so viewed him? Why, Catherine Morland. At the start of their acquaintance Catherine fears "that he indulged himself a little too much with the foibles of others", while she listens to the grave assent he confers upon Mrs. Allen's divulgings as to the properties of muslin and the amenities of Bath. In their first conversation he has been busily running intellectual rings round Catherine to his own complete satisfaction and gratification, if not hers: diverting her with Assembly Room chatter and posturings, teasing her with what she might privately think of him, and enthusing upon the perfection of women's letter-writing save for the three characteristics of its deficiency of subject, inattention to punctuation and ignorance of grammar.

With what delighted energy he pounces upon any infelicity in Catherine's speech. Her pleonastic concept of a "faithful promise" from Isabella Thorpe receives, perhaps, the short shrift it merits. But her undiscriminating use of "nice" is met with open ridicule; and her declaring that she has "just learnt to love a hyacinth" by the mockingly ironical, "And how might you learn? – By accident or argument?"

The spirited humour of Henry's upbraidings seems to free them from offence. Who could really be solemn about his protestation, on being charged to state his acknowledgement of women's intelligence, that "no one can think more highly of the understanding of women than I do. In my opinion, nature has given them so much, that they never find it necessary to use more than half". And we dismiss it as brotherly banter when he sports with Eleanor's alarmed incomprehension of Catherine's prophecy that "something very shocking indeed" – by which she means an horrific novel – "will soon come out in London". "Forgive her stupidity", he urges Catherine. "The fears of the sister have added to the weakness of the woman; but she is by no means a simpleton in general".

This trenchancy may, however, be somewhat less agreeable – bring in asperity of tone, and manner bordering on the inquisitorial, as for example in Henry's relentless questioning upon finding Catherine in an unexpected part of the Abbey. But the cleverness which discomfits her then can, on occasion, be too much even for himself. When he is driving her to Northanger, he diverts her with an extempore Gothic tale so compelling that he has to break off through being able no longer to "command solemnity of subject or voice". His very triumph in the jest incapacitates him. To adapt a definition from a different context, he becomes inebriated with the exuberance of his own virtuosity.

What symptoms are these but of pride in high intelligence: of a self-congratulation on his own brilliancy in the style of Shakespeare's Benedick? But while Benedick meets his match in both senses in Beatrice, Tilney is properly vanquished by his very antithesis in Catherine Morland. As Jane Austen coolly remarks as to their encounter,

> Where people wish to attach, they should always be ignorant. To come with a well-informed mind, is to come with an inability of administering to the vanity of others, which a sensible person would always wish to avoid. A woman especially, if she have the misfortune of knowing any thing, should conceal it as well as she can.

Catherine has no cleverness to conceal from Henry, and no art to conceal it if she possessed it. Not for nothing is she made to reply, when he declares that he understands her perfectly, "Me? – yes; I cannot speak well enough to be unintelligible". Her entire response to him is an innocent flattery: in his company she is "listening with sparkling eyes to every thing he said; and, in finding him irresistible, becoming so herself". When, therefore, he comes to propose to her, he is soliciting a heart "which, perhaps, they pretty equally knew was already entirely his own". His is a deep and true affection; but as to its origin, we are told "that a persuasion of her partiality for him had been the only cause of giving her a serious thought". He loves Catherine for those fine attributes which flow from unpretentiousness in human nature – but also, to some degree at least, because she is, and happily cannot help being, a living confirmation of his high opinion of himself.

Henry Crawford is not the hero of the novel, but he might well have been. When that other Henry, Jane Austen's brother, got to book three of *Mansfield Park*, he thought that Crawford might win Fanny Price in the end; and we owe to Margaret Kennedy the insight that he would have made a better husband for someone of her qualities than Edmund Bertram[17]. And yet the author shows us that vanity, pure and simple, is largely determinative of his actions and hopes. The giving free rein to it accounts for his characteristic unwillingness to look beyond the present moment, and his consequent drifting course through the story. It explains also his arid relations with Maria and Julia Bertram. The sisters "were an amusement to his sated mind": his pleasure in their company stems from the deeper joy he evinces in the adroit exercise of his engaging powers, in conferring attentions sufficient to attract both girls while never seeming directed at either. Jane Austen's term for behaviour of this type is "to trifle"; and what could better describe the blandishments Crawford bestows on Maria that day at Sotherton Court? It is vanity, again, or pique arising from its frustration, which provokes him to gain the satisfaction of "making a small hole in Fanny's heart": for despite his best efforts he had unaccountably got nowhere with her. Attempting it he finds himself, more unaccountably, in love for the first time. But he brings to the task of courtship a mind "sanguine and pre-assured", which can first imagine affection to exist beneath Fanny's manifest indifference, and then find "so much delight in the idea of obliging her to love him in a very short time, that her not loving him now was scarcely regretted". It cannot at any stage enter his thoughts that "Love such as his, in a man like himself", should ever fail of a return.

Crawford is the perpetrator of what perhaps is the most fulsome act of incivility in the novels. While Lady Bertram peacefully slumbers on the drawing room sofa at Mansfield, and Edmund, indulgently taking what is going on to be the lovers' tiff that it is not, hides himself in a newspaper, Crawford remorselessly cross-examines the helpless Fanny

Price as to her impression of him. He persists in forcing a confidence in utter disregard of her embarrassment, anguished feelings, and appeals – and in defiance of manners, as of manliness. For rudeness is none other than the external indication of people's being wrapped up in and existing for themselves.

And it is vanity which brings Crawford to his ruin. He loves Fanny still; but the same compulsion which led him first to exert his charm upon her obliges him to try to re-animate Maria's former regard when they meet at Mrs. Fraser's party, and he is received by her with dismissive coldness. He is, we are told,

> mortified, he could not bear to be thrown off by the woman whose smiles had been so wholly at his command; he must assert himself to subdue so proud a display of resentment.

So he begins the attack in which he is overwhelmed by the strength of feelings in Maria Bertram beyond what he had supposed to exist. The self-concern which so aided him in his trifling had been all along deluding him as to the realities of relationship. A justice of inexorable consequence brings it about, therefore, that at the end, "He was entangled by his own vanity".

Anyone listing the instances through the novel of conduct in Crawford deriving from this feature of his personality would find they had something like the outline of an allegorical figure from a Morality play. But there is nothing abstract about Henry Crawford: with his manifold accomplishments he is solidly human – all too human. If, nonetheless, his portrayal should offer the least suggestion of the Morality, it will be neither as Vice nor Vanity, but, alas, much nearer an Everyman.

There is no point in looking for pride and vanity in Edward Ferrars. A stern critic might say it is not easy to find much else, or wonder in the common phrase what Elinor sees in him. But so culpable an innocence could be the legacy of two disadvantages he almost throughout labours under: that of being engaged to another according to the strict standards of the times, and that of being without fortune and thus dependent on a parent's whim. That the rigours and inhibitions of the latter state are not readily discerned today is hardly surprising, when they could escape the notice of contemporaries. Emma Woodhouse can admonish her friend with, "You are the worst judge in the world, Mr. Knightley, of the difficulties of dependence". Its disabling force is perhaps visible in Captain Tilney, upon his father's denouncing him for coming down late to breakfast. He listens in silence, attempts no defence; and, we learn, Catherine "scarcely heard his voice while his father remained in the room,…so much were his spirits affected". Making allowance for the restrictions Edward Ferrars finds himself under permits one to think there could be more to him than meets the eye. The contrasting effusiveness of his younger brother is explainable as simply the token of Robert's deeper kinship in stupidity with his all-powerful mother.

But there is not the slightest prospect of Edward Ferrars' bearing comparison with Frederick Wentworth, the most heroic of Jane Austen's heroes: a man, according to Margaret Kennedy, "completely masculine in all he says and does"[18]. If this is so – and few would deny it – should there not be found in him a correspondingly greater impulsion, typical of his gender, to look well in his own eyes, or in the eyes of others, or both? Wentworth does, in fact, contrive to leave the inhabitants of the Great House at Uppercross in no doubt as to his abilities. He talks happily and unrestrainedly about his doings: about his "taking privateers enough to be very entertaining" when in command of the Asp, and of having "such a lovely cruise" off the Western Islands in the Laconia. "How fast I made money in her!" he assures the assembled party. – But you've to be careful with a man like this. When you consider that these expressions "entertaining", "lovely", and "making money" are euphemisms for fights at sea, and that he is giving very keen listeners an account of events, and making no bones about it, in the manner of any sailor telling a yarn, you find you are in the presence of something that merits respect. If there is a trace of vanity in Wentworth's disposition to talk freely of his exploits, it is the product, at least, of exceptional achievement. He wouldn't be human if he were not conscious of personal claim and merit: in Charlotte Lucas's words, "If I may so express it, he has a *right* to be proud". It would never come into his mind, though, to use this implied prerogative for the purpose of boasting. We know it would be quite beneath him; and we are left with the fact of Wentworth's natural impressiveness.

This fact, perhaps, is mainly responsible for the singular lapse on his part with respect to the Miss Musgroves – a fault for which Ann Elliot, predisposed as she is in his favour, knows not how to excuse him. "He was only wrong", she concludes, "in accepting the attentions – (for accepting must be the word) of two young women at once". But he had hardly been acting by design, and is shocked when the import becomes clear. The involvement is one which seems to have grown around him in the general warmth of regard at Uppercross, there being "so much of friendliness, and of flattery, and of every thing most bewitching in his reception there". Indeed, Jane Austen queries, "If he were a little spoilt by such universal, such eager admiration, who could wonder?" While Wentworth is blamable for his insensitivity, his willingness to bear the consequence frees him from discredit.

When, eight years after their broken engagement, he had come to stay with the Crofts at Kellynch Hall, Ann Elliot wondered what his wishes were with respect to meeting her again. She tries to work them out by adopting his standpoint and reasoning from it.

> Had he wished ever to see her again [she tells herself] he need not have waited till this time; he would have done what she could not but believe that in his place she should have done long ago, when events had been early giving him the independence which alone had been wanting.

Her conclusion is that therefore, "He must be either indifferent or unwilling". But in this she is wrong: the very opposite is true. She is in error on a vital matter, simply because it is a woman's mind that she has employed upon it. As a woman she knows of nothing that would have prevented her from renewing acquaintance if she had desired to; it takes a man to make her aware of what the impediment had been – the man being Wentworth himself. During the card party at Camden Place, when they have drawn aside from the other guests, he asks her the very question she had posed to herself: would she have renewed the engagement if he had written after a couple of years? And her smiling response draws from him a passionate confession not only as to his wishes, but as to his nature.

> "It is not that I did not think of it, or desire it, as what could alone crown all my other success. But I was proud, too proud to ask again."

Self-esteem in Wentworth issued the command which had to be obeyed, in defiance of every other appeal of his being. The whole story of *Persuasion* displays the reality and consequence of masculine pride.

\*   \*   \*

By this stage some will be saying, "Wait a moment. What's going on? An insidious attempt, it would seem, to typify Jane Austen's men – excellent fellows – as pitifully presuming and vainglorious sorts of creatures. Is this to be endured?" So, before I am drummed out of the regiment, let me hasten to say that the women in principle are just as bad. Think of Lady Catherine sallying forth to confront the fractious residents of Hunsford, and "settle their differences, silence their complaints, and scold them into harmony and plenty" by that awesome sincerity and frankness for which her character has ever been celebrated. With some slight adjustment of rank (overdue, without doubt, in her estimation), would she not make a fitting consort for a monarch, and be heard declaring herself, "Ay, every inch a queen", as with complacency she perceives the trembling of her subjects? Or consider Mrs. Elton, a parvenue in Highbury, presuming to detach the social initiative from its rightful and incensed custodian, with her,

"Miss Woodhouse, we must exert ourselves", and her detestable "You and I's". Isn't it the first article of her faith that she is wonderful? And this applies to the Miss Bertrams, who were popular wherever they went because "Their vanity was in such good order, that they seemed to be quite free from it, and gave themselves no airs", as it does to Mary Musgrove, whose tenacity about the deference due to her as a baronet's daughter is constantly causing annoyance even among those close to her.

Yes, Jane Austen's women are as vain and proud as the men in principle – but not quite so in fact. Not because they are better, but merely because it was, and is, harder for a woman to fulfil the requirements of self-magnification. They are not really compatible with the feminine role of bringing harmony, social and musical, into the life of the household; or that of bearing children; or of dealing with demanding husbands enjoying a freedom they were denied. And, to a woman's quicker and finer sensibilities, the very notion of glorifying the self will tend to appear a little suspect. Her duties and perceptions alike are of a humbling kind: and the more salutary for being so.

This, presumably, is why an American professorial friend once confided to me that he had no trouble choosing whom to vote for in an election. "If there's a woman candidate, I vote for her, regardless of party". His explanation was as follows: "Because it's impossible for a woman to be worse than the men; and there's a slight chance she might be better".

And this is also the reason why Jane Austen, who is not strictly a satirist, here and there allows herself the luxury of parodying her own male characters. You hear its ring in the protestations of the necessitous Sir Walter Elliot that, "It had not been possible for him to spend less; he had done nothing but what Sir Walter Elliot was imperiously called on to do; but blameless as he was", and so on. But it is at Mansfield Parsonage, in the course of one of Sir Thomas Bertram's "dignified musings", this time upon attentions Fanny Price appears to be receiving, that the mimicry is more pronounced.

> ...though infinitely above scheming or contriving for any the most advantageous matrimonial establishment that could be among the possibilities of any one most dear to him, and disdaining even as a littleness the being quick-sighted on such points, he could not avoid perceiving in a grand and careless way that Mr. Crawford was somewhat distinguishing his niece.

That she will parody wherever it is merited, regardless of sex, is delightfully demonstrated in the set-piece of Mrs. Elton's dulcet utterances amidst Donwell Abbey's strawberry-beds. But the men more aptly incur such ridicule because of her knowledge that they are more inclined than women to build a pretentious and brittle self-image, and that in this respect they are vulnerable, and women stronger.

For proof one has only to compare the quarrel between Anne and Elizabeth Elliot in *Persuasion* with that between Edmund and Tom Bertram in *Mansfield Park*. The circumstances are similar. In both, the younger tries to warn and advise the elder about a course of conduct which could be personally and socially harmful: in the one case, embarking on amateur theatricals in Sir Thomas's absence, and in the other, permitting the commoner Mrs. Clay to remain a member of the household. But for the sisters the issue is far more serious. Tom Bertram risks no more than arousing his father's and the neighbourhood's displeasure; but what threatens Elizabeth is not only the disgrace of complicity in Sir Walter's marrying beneath him, but loss of all her rights as mistress of Kellynch Hall, and even at Camden Place.

Yet where most is at stake, there is least offence given or taken. Elizabeth, vexed by the reflection on her judgment and what she must regard as an upstart endeavour in Anne, conveys her displeasure in answers of shortness and warmth. But, compared to what takes place between the brothers, the combat is ceremonious, the exchanges ritual. Anger seems to have been at once anticipated; it is allowed for, and promptly dismissed: the contenders part confirmed, naturally, in their own attitudes, but unshaken and unscathed.

With the men it is otherwise. Although annoyance is as much as possible dissimulated at the behest of good breeding, there is nothing ceremonious about their encounter. Tom, in surprise and irritation at the challenge, from the start makes a defiantly contradictory riposte: to the plea of Maria's delicate situation it is, "I have no fears, and no scruples"; to the argument that his father will disapprove, "And I am convinced to the contrary". When Edmund persists in urging Sir Thomas's strong sense of decorum, Tom is, in Jane Austen's understated term, "displeased". His answer is a scathing affirmation of his status as Mansfield's heir and acting head that shows him touched to the quick. "I'll take care that his daughters do nothing to distress him. Manage your own concerns, Edmund, and I'll take care of the rest of the family". Against his brother's charge that staging a play would be taking liberties with his father's house, Tom, "in a decided tone", attempts a studied sarcasm. "His house shall not be hurt. I have quite as great an interest in being careful of his house as you can have". But vehemence and ridicule bursts forth in his cries of "Absolute nonsense!" and of "prodigious!" at the likely expense; and the last, as he walks out of the room, is plain denunciation. "Don't imagine that nobody in this house can see or judge but yourself. Don't act yourself if you do not like it, but don't expect to govern every body else".

There's no mistaking it. Here are the throbbings, the whirls and eddies of humiliation and pain: both young men experience raw emotions which bring them near the limit of the tolerable. It is with an image of animal savagery that the author, appropriately, concludes this scene. "Family squabbling is the greatest evil of all", Edmund confides to Fanny Price, "and we had better do any thing than be altogether by the ears". One wonders how things would have gone if she had not been there; but even with her present, Jane Austen is revealing a man's world to us – and the depth of her understanding of the male ego. For it is wounded vanity and pride which makes this quarrel so much more damaging than the other. Not that women don't also have their pride: it is just that in their natures pride tends not to dominate.

*   *   *

Love, rather, preponderates with women, does it not? – a thing apart in the lives of men, but for women their whole existence, if Byron is to be believed. Surely, men are in this respect the hardier, the less susceptible? Only an affirmative, seemingly, can come from the novels, for the sentiments of woman are Jane Austen's main theme: she will not normally enter into male preserves, or much into the minds of her male characters. The tendernesses and apprehensions of love and falling in love are registered in all her heroines, and its pains movingly displayed in a Marianne Dashwood – or in an Anne Elliot, when she undergoes "All the overpowering, blinding, bewildering first effects of strong surprise" upon glimpsing Captain Wentworth in Milsom Street. But perturbation is also apparent in Wentworth as, seconds later, he recognizes her. It is described from without; yet the words, "He was more obviously struck and confused by the sight of her, than she had ever observed before" convey a great deal – as does Darcy's similar reaction to Elizabeth upon his encountering her at Pemberley.

Are Jane Austen's men to any extent freer from love's tyranny than her women? Is the passion less potent or compelling for them? It is a hard question, as Anne Elliot and Captain Harville find in their conversation at the White Hart. But a parallel may be drawn between the pathetic state of Marianne Dashwood and that of Edmund Bertram, who, under love's constraining, is through much of the novel a shadow of the man he was. He becomes a creature of desperate confessions and confidences, the agonized victim, even, of every new token of Mary Crawford's inclining towards him, or otherwise. Rarely can the horror of a perceived imperfection in the beloved have found such expression as it does in him. "She does not *think* evil", he tells Fanny, "but she speaks it – speaks it in playfulness – and though I know it to be playfulness, it grieves me to the soul". Nor can the predicament of the anxious lover have been often better exemplified. Despite all his self-knowledge, and knowledge of Mary's failings, he knows not how to come to terms with his promptings or settle on a purposive action, and is left clinging to fitful hope like a drowning man to a straw. – Or we might take note of Harville himself, speaking from his soul of a love which for him is in no sense a thing apart; whose one wish – words failing as they must, and his composure with them – is that he might convey "all that a man can bear and do, and glories to do for the sake of these treasures of his existence!"

It is, though, the ending of that discussion at the White Hart which would appear to be decisive. Love's like hold upon men is not to be doubted, at least – to use Anne Elliot's words – "while the woman you love lives, and lives for you". She claims for her sex what she calls an unenviable privilege, which Harville cannot bring himself to deny her: "that of loving longest, when existence or when hope is gone". But there is more than a hint of the privilege's not being woman's alone, in, of all people, Willoughby – the man who has knowingly sported with Marianne's affections, and discarded her as deliberately, to marry upon financial consideration a woman he does not care for. His precipitate journey to Somerset upon news of Marianne's dangerous illness may have a touch of bravado about it, as may his manner to Elinor during their strange interview at Cleveland that stormy night; but what quickly becomes clear is the bitter thoughts and torturing regret which animate him. Realization of his true state softens Elinor – more, moves her beyond pity to the near-affection which she has to struggle against. But it is Willoughby's final plea which is most instructive. He desires to know that Marianne has forgiven him. He is assured, with sympathy, that she has. But he wants something beyond this: to be able to fancy, as he puts it, that "a better knowledge of my heart, and of my present feelings, will draw from her a more spontaneous, more natural, more gentle, less dignified, forgiveness".

Only love itself could so wish, so crave, so rejoice in such a relenting, in one for ever separated – could find her regard still so infinitely meaningful when hope is at an end. Anne Elliot's assertion on behalf of her sex of loving longest well attests her own constancy, and gives Captain Wentworth, as he sits writing at the nearby table, the intimation vital for its finding a return. But the claim she makes is one which Jane Austen, from her own observation of love in men and women, knows to be untrue.

\* \* \*

This awareness of equality between men and women where the profoundest instincts of the heart are evoked might seem hard to reconcile with a disparity in the presentation of the sexes in the novels. Jane Austen certainly appears to devote less attention to her men, and depicts them almost invariably from external vision. But that her achievement in characterization is more pronounced with women has more to do with the obligation she was under of conformity with her generation's idea of the novel, than with lesser ability in delineating men, by whatever method. In Mr. Bennet, if not elsewhere, we assuredly have a demonstration of the extent of her powers. Elizabeth Jenkins sets it down as "next door to impossible" for him to have been created by a woman. His having been drawn by a man would be more credible, she goes on, "except that it is difficult to think of a man who could have drawn him so well"[19]. We have all been entertained by the idiosyncrasy that expresses itself now in a distant and dismissive courtesy, now in elaborate irony and sarcasm, now in a judicial expansiveness, as occasion serves; and we are aware of the sudden impatience, and the capacity for fierce self-reproach and momentary gloom which belongs to a personality at once forceful and withdrawn. But nowhere else in the novels – and, one suspects, in anyone else's novels – do we come upon such chameleon-like change of attitude as occurs in Mr. Bennet when he is challenged to the depth of his being by his favourite daughter's seeming abandonment of her standards, in suddenly wanting to marry the man she has hitherto hated.

"What are you doing? Are you out of your senses, to be accepting this man?" he asks her, in shock and grief. But his mood, as Elizabeth rather confusedly assures him of her attachment, is instantly that of disdain. "Or in other words", he puts it to her, "you are determined to have him. He is rich, to be sure". Upon her steadfastly declaring her love for Darcy, Elizabeth hears accents of the tenderest fatherly concern. He has given Darcy his consent; he is prepared to give it to her; but, forewarning of the miseries of an unsuitable match, he pleads, "My child, let me not have the grief of seeing *you* unable to respect your partner in life. You know not what you are about". It is he, however, who is prevailed on to think again when Elizabeth, much moved, explains the change which has come about in herself, and urges Darcy's constancy and his good qualities. Bennet, still unconvinced, gives grudging approval: "I have no more to say. If this be the case, he deserves you". The tone is now that of resigned disappointment; but as Elizabeth recounts what Darcy has done for Lydia, it transmutes itself into elation. "And so Darcy did everything; made up the match, gave the money, paid the fellow's debts, and got him his commission!" There follows, in rapid succession, relief blended with humour: "So much the better. It will save me a world of trouble and economy"; an outburst of hilarity, as he laughs "some time" at Elizabeth over her earlier embarrassment at the warnings against Darcy in Mr. Collins's letter; and, finally, a comfortable relapse into the ironic courtesy of his customary manner: "If any young men come for Mary or Kitty, send them in, for I am quite at leisure".

The most fanciful and volatile of womankind in the novels could scarcely display such variation of mood. Yet these manifold states are truly Mr. Bennet: in them all, he is consistently himself, behaving exactly as we would expect him to behave – and entirely masculine. By no stretch of the imagination can his conduct (to use Elizabeth's previous words about her father) "be mistaken for the affectation and coquetry of an elegant female". And in none of her heroines does Jane Austen evince a greater triumph of comprehension.

She is as successful with men as with women in the concise rendering of character. The description of Mrs. Bennet as "a woman of mean understanding, little information, and uncertain temper" sets us smiling, and speaks eloquently. More might be held to devolve from the single point of taciturnity in Mrs. Ferrars: "She was not a woman of many words: for, unlike people in general, she proportioned them to the number of her ideas". This piece of summarizing does not, however, outdo her performance with respect to Sir William Lucas and Sir Walter Elliot – or in Admiral Croft's illuminating self-caricature through speeches like, "A new sort of way this, for a young fellow to be making love, by breaking his mistress's head! – is not it, Miss Elliot? – This is breaking a head and giving a plaister truly!" But her introduction of John Thorpe perhaps exceeds these in inspired inventiveness. This plain, rather stout individual "seemed fearful of being too handsome unless he wore the dress of a groom, and too much like a gentleman unless he were easy where he ought to be civil, and impudent where he might be allowed to be easy". The man's native worth, and the manner of his subsequent conduct, are alike deducible from this searing definition.

Not only her men's differentiation, but their similarity, can prove the measure of Jane Austen's skill. In a notable respect they are less outwardly distinguished from one another than their counterparts among the ladies. By air and accent, Charles Musgrove, Edmund Bertram, Edward Ferrars, Charles Bingley and Edward Gardiner are not easy to tell apart. They share the unassuming matter-of-factness and moderation which typified the country gentlemen of Jane Austen's personal acquaintance. Nevertheless, they are quite unlike as individuals: each seems to exist within a unique mental climate. The fact denotes an extraordinary sureness of touch.

So also does the variety of splendidly realized male types to be found in the novels. They are as abundant as those of the women; and comparison will show that for most female categories there is a male equivalent. For that of mindlessness and vacuity, we may have the agreeable occupation of choosing between Lady Bertram and Mrs. Allen on the one side, and Sir William Lucas and Mr. Rushworth on the other. When it comes to egotism and the will to dominate, Lady Catherine and General Tilney have much in common; some of his performances might conceivably be deemed to outclass hers. The principled and deliberative personality is at least as well exemplified in Sir Thomas Bertram as it is in Lady Russell. If the comportment of Mrs. Weston may (as Emma maintains) be regarded as the model of "propriety, simplicity, and elegance" in a female, that of Mr. Gardiner for much the same reason is to be recommended to any man. In terms of what is avowedly ladylike and gentlemanly, Anne Elliot and Mr. Knightley would appear to be outstanding; and if Mrs. Grant merits praise for the preservation of cheerfulness despite being married to a perverse husband, Charles Musgrove, espoused to a fretful wife, is the man so distinguished.

Vulgarity, as Jane Austen was all too aware, is a plant which can never cease to flourish; and many, amidst its convoluted branches, share an exotic relationship. Those fine cronies, Mrs. Jennings and Sir John Middleton, are not alone in displaying a consanguinity defiant of the widest divergence in the social scale: the gushing Anne Steele and vaunting Robert Ferrars are likewise linked in the species of vulgarity that feeds upon silliness and finds fulfilment in garrulity. That which is the mere offspring of underbreeding is demonstrated by the siblings Isabella and John Thorpe respectively in their consummate coquetry and rattledom; while the sort produced unawares by those engaged in the nefarious art of social posturing and pretence is personified in Mrs. Elton and her *caro sposo*.

But, human nature being what it is, gentility itself can carry the seeds of infelicities too numerous to recount; and many are the ramifications of those who, endowed with manners, yet sin against them. Some contrive to do so by excess, like Sir Walter and Elizabeth, in whom may be observed the self-congratulating haughtiness which can freeze a crowded room into silence, or the adulation of rank that makes Anne Elliot so oddly wish that her family had more pride. Far from being a garb of innocence, manners can mask the duplicity of the mercenary predator, a creature as well represented amongst the men by Wickham and Willoughby as it is by Mrs. Clay and – yes, it must be said, Charlotte Lucas amongst the women. Mannerliness may even beget a blatant self-assurance which spurns the very intimations that give it life: Marianne Dashwood and Willoughby have both indulged in this refined abandon.

For representatives of that ease and cleverness in otherwise charming people which can be tempted into the reprehensible, one need look no further than to Emma Woodhouse and Frank Churchill. When the deceptions he secretly so much enjoyed are known and forgiven, she makes a statement for which he has no other answer than a bow of assent: "to tell you the truth, I think it might have been some amusement to myself in the same situation. I think there is a little likeness between us". They are so alike in this that it is well they go separate ways. And of the rather more questionable quipping and quibbling propensity, which twenty thousand pounds and the assurance it gives has created in Mary Crawford, we have as positive a masculine representation in the jovial irresponsibility and barbed outspokenness which comes so naturally to Tom Bertram as elder son. His observing that the "desperate dull life her's must be with the doctor" shows Mrs. Grant's dire need of a lover, and Mary's likening Maria's marriage and Edmund's ordination upon Sir Thomas's return from abroad to sacrificial offerings made to some heathen deity, are about equal in irreverence, if not quite so in ingenuity. That the paths of this pair diverge is also, one must think, probably a merciful provision.

But Miss Bates and Mr. Woodhouse are eternally neighbours and friends, twin and potent reminders as they are of how socially disastrous good nature can be if unaccompanied by both of two other needful complementary qualities. Miss Bates has perception in plenty, but not the least discretion; in Mr. Woodhouse is a teeming discretion that is without any perception to work upon. As characters they are not too ossified to be compatible: put together, they get on famously – though, curiously enough, not without a little straining of good nature on either side. For whereas she must grieve at his not letting her eat the delicacies put before her at Hartfield, he is driven to confessing with some irritation that she talks a little too quick.

For some of course there is not a corresponding person of the other sex. There is to be found no woman like Admiral Croft in his endearing and sometimes alarming breeziness – or man comparable to Lydia Bennet, "this robust, noisy, natural creature", as she has been called[20]. Mrs. Norris also is without a masculine counterpart in her presumption and petulance as indigent sister. Similarly, it is pointless looking for a true female version of Mr. Collins, for the reason that women are simply not capable of being so obtuse. And there is no gentleman remotely resembling Mrs. Bennet – but who on earth would expect one? The striking thing, however, about these novels concerned with the amours of women is the range of male characters drawn from many social conditions they set before us.

\*   \*   \*

One category makes what might be thought an improbable appearance: that of the evil man. In *Lady Susan*, Jane Austen had drawn a wicked woman who pursues her designs with cold subtlety; General Tilney betrays a malevolence crude and unrestrained. But use of such terms in relation to him can readily appear an exaggeration. Is he not, after all, something of a joke, designedly and actually: a character whose purpose is to show Catherine being so naively under the influence of Mrs. Radcliffe's Gothic horrors as to suppose the General, "slowly pacing the drawing-room for an hour together in silent thoughtfulness, with downcast eyes and contracted brow", another villainous Montoni, when he is merely thinking over the latest batch of political papers and pamphlets – and turning out, in the end, to be no more than a petulent old buffer, anyway?

Henry Tilney is right when he accuses Catherine of having formed a surmise of such horror as makes him at a loss for words. The General is innocent of the despicable murder she had suspected him of; but we should be unwise to dismiss those suspicions as idle without giving some thought to what they are grounded on. At an early stage Catherine is aware of an effect seemingly without cause. General Tilney's children are oppressed in his company; and she herself finds it "a release to get away from him", despite his pointed courtesies. Indeed, it is through his absence, Jane Austen declares, that she derives "the first experimental conviction that a loss may be sometimes a gain".

Catherine finds nothing sinister in the incidents of their journey to Northanger – his wrath about the carriage, "his discontent at whatever the inn afforded, and his angry impatience at the waiters" – but accepts them as the given fact of a life-style she is unfamiliar with. Though this brand of assertiveness compares strangely with the civility which can rise to such height of compliment as beg her, while in Bath, to "quit this scene of public triumph" in order to be his guest, and bestow on her "one of the most graceful bows she had ever beheld", it does not detract from her pleasure in being so honoured, or cause her to fancy a hollowness in his attentions.

Might she not have sensed pride of possession, at least, beneath the mock-modesty which could concede the Abbey's palatial dining room to be "by no means an ill-sized room", and the apologetic of, "Why, as he *had* such rooms, he thought it would be simple not to make use of them"? And was she at all led to wonder at the persistence of the Generals's questioning about her friend Mr. Allen's rooms, his garden, and his succession houses, as he showed her round his own – or, on her assuring him of their inferiority, at his exclaiming of Mr. Allen, "'He is a happy man!' with a look of very happy contempt"?

The answers must be in the negative. It would have been beyond Catherine, in her innocence, to make anything of the evidence which even the accomplished reader is disinclined to take in: evidence of a fierce hunger for distinction, a huge gratification in its attainment, and a consonant apprehension of its loss which puts him instantly on the defensive at the slightest hint of criticism. But astonished she is when, after his urging Henry to go to no trouble in receiving him at Woodston, that "Whatever you may happen to have in the house will be enough", she sees the festive abundance there which he attacks with such obvious inconsistency and relish.

Little does Catherine know that General Tilney's condescension towards her has been of the same quality as these other manifestations: called forth, that is, by exultant anticipation of receiving an heiress into the family in her person. The full force of his disappointment in this prospect she is soon to feel in his suddenly turning her out of the house; but her own distress at this juncture is somewhat less than the General's. The being informed that she is a virtual pauper has, Jane Austen states, "terrified" him. Even this calculated use of the word cannot convey the enormity of such an assault upon such a mind. Here is a man whose manners are in every respect artifice, beneath whose outward politeness broods a barren nature swept by storms of passion: blind will to dominate, zest in self-assertion, greed to possess, rage at hindrance to a wish, – and, underlying all, the primordial fear, adjunct of unhallowed condition, which lends intensity to these malign satisfactions and strivings.

We may smile at Catherine's detecting a Montoni in Henry's father. He is, beyond denial, as his son rather aggrievedly points out, an English gentleman and a Christian. But were it to be removed from its particular environment and culture and placed under a less favoured dispensation, this personality would quickly decline upon its native barbarism. The best thing Catherine does in the novel is to fall in love with Henry Tilney: the next best is to develop the revulsion towards the General she feels almost throughout.

Another piece of remarkable veracity, though of quite different sort, may reside in the character of Mr. Darcy and his treatment of Elizabeth Bennet. His specifying and detailing to her the social inferiority of her family in the midst of proposing has been deemed unlikely conduct in a hero. Darcy appears to be sinning against the manners and decorum of the age, and against probability in a person of his type: what he might have thought, that is, it would never have occurred to him to speak. The seeming lapse has been explained by critics, the present one included, as due to Jane Austen's need to make Darcy at this moment the embodiment of the arrogance of rank and wealth she deplores, and her contriving to do so through an action uncharacteristic in someone like him. But is it uncharacteristic? Is there not such a thing as the pride which will not stoop to dissembling – and the constraint to be true to oneself in a searching encounter? Darcy's is an aloofness of spirit, as well as of attitude. And given, further, that uprightness and even severity of mind which can pronounce, at such a point, "disguise of every sort is my abhorrence!" and the ardour for truth and scorn of pretence in Elizabeth which Darcy has recognized and holds in esteem, might it not rather be that the "understanding" of a coming-together between such a pair can scarcely subsist without a real understanding of each other's position?

At least it may be said without contradiction that Darcy tells her not a thing about her family's deficiencies and shortcomings that she does not know and has not ruefully acknowledged to herself – though it is inevitable that she will react with anger to the open breach of decorum his candour is. Nor can it be denied that Darcy by this forthrightness succeeds in apprising Elizabeth of the reality of his love for her. Almost immediately she is experiencing a different form of agitation at the thought of having "inspired unconsciously so strong an affection".

Far from dealing here with an artificiality of characterization, we are being confronted with a phenomenal naturalness. There can be no swervings or zigzaggings of politeness with these two when it comes to matters so close to the heart, and to principle: such "mannerliness" would itself have been an artificiality in terms of the people they are. The plainness Darcy uses, and desires, in proposing to Elizabeth at the end proclaims the man: "You are too generous", be tells her, "to trifle with me". That their married life will, indeed, never be a refuge from home truths is indicated soon thereafter by the style of this newly-betrothed young woman's complaisance towards her beloved, when, inquiring what had made him begin to be in love with her, she points out, with devastating frankness, "My beauty you had early withstood". Can it be that in Elizabeth Bennet we have another Lady Catherine de Bourgh in the making? Perish the thought! Hers is too intelligent and responsive a mind to incur such a destiny. But in this connection it would appear that Elizabeth has found in Darcy, not just her man, but her soul-mate.

Should some hesitate to accept this reading of Mr. Darcy, on the grounds that, whatever might be pleaded in extenuation, no true gentleman could have behaved so, they may be advised to dismiss their scruple as they can. And to rid themselves permanently of the notion all they need do is devote the odd hour to researching confrontations of Whig and Tory in the House of Commons.

\* \* \*

Darcy, Knightley, Wentworth, Bertram, Tilney – even Ferrars: each is markedly individual: yet do they together represent an ideal of manliness for Jane Austen? What, to conclude, are the attributes in men she seems most to approve? Answers will be easily forthcoming, since they are embodied in the gentlemen themselves; but nothing can be better at the outset than to take note of Elizabeth's plea to Mr. Collins, that he regard her as "a rational creature speaking the truth from her heart". The heroes shun the established complimentary mode of address that sets women in a separate and subordinate class. In contrast to the strained gallantry of Mr. Elton, which made Emma want to run away and laugh, there is placed before us with obvious approval the manner towards Mary Crawford and women in general of Edmund Bertram: "he was not pleasant by any common rule, he talked no nonsense, he paid no compliments, his opinions were unbending, his attentions tranquil and simple".

Equally demanded, we may gather, is the capacity in a man to laugh at himself or tolerate being laughed at. The latter we are assured Mr. Darcy will gravitate towards; but both exist in Mr. Knightley, the former being overlaid by a magisterial outspokenness. Therefore we should not miss the chuckle when, in advising Emma to obtain from Harriet those "minute particulars" of her engagement to Robert Martin "which only woman's language can make interesting", he adds on behalf of men, "In our communications we deal only in the great". And Frederick Wentworth, wishing to impress upon Louisa Musgrove the desirability of firmness, and by way of illustration plucking a perfect nut from a bough, next moment is brought by sudden sense of incongruity to refer to it as being "still in possession of all the happiness that a hazel-nut can be supposed capable of ". In a woman, a sense of humour is an attraction; but for a man it is, according to Jane Austen's thinking, a prerequisite.

So is integrity in human dealings. It is the knowledge of its presence in Mr. Knightley which allows Emma at once to dismiss the thought of his being the giver of the unexplained present of a piano to Jane Fairfax. He would, she is sure, never have acted in so devious a way. And the revelation of Frank Churchill's past course of double-dealing consequent upon the secret engagement rouses Emma to condemnation in Mrs. Weston's very presence, so horrified is she at the thought of the absence in him of "that upright integrity, that strict adherence to truth and principle, that disdain of trick and littleness, which a man should display in every transaction of his life". She voices here the mind of her creator, all of whose heroes are typified by a principled directness. So are they by a readiness to accept responsibility for their mistakes or impulsive actions. Having allowed his attentions to Louisa Musgrove to appear too meaningful, Wentworth is resigned. "I was hers in honour if she wanted it", he says. "I had been unguarded". In the same way, Henry Tilney will take it upon himself to atone for his father's clear favouritism and subsequent gross misconduct towards Catherine: to her "He felt himself bound as much in honour as in affection", we are informed.

Such probity is part of the good manners always requisite in a man. They go beyond the politeness observable at surface level; and even there they are not admissible if they express elaborateness rather than the simplicity that is itself befitting, in its betokening the sincere. Manners do, of course, involve some pretence – a masking for social convenience, if not repressing, of genuine feeling, as when Wentworth responds to Mary Musgrove's depreciation of her relatives the Hayters with "an artificial, assenting smile, followed by a contemptuous glance, as he turned away". It is a requirement of good manners also not to defy public opinion "in any point of worldly decorum": and here, Marianne's flaunting "particularity" with Willoughby shows her utterly in the wrong. But, as her sister so earnestly tries to impress on her, such abiding by the conventions does not mean allowing them to prevail over personal belief or taste. It is on the contrary imperative, especially in a man, to be able while respecting society's norms and refinements to see beyond them, and where appropriate act accordingly – above all with regard to the human worth which might perhaps fall short of them, and to the human arrogance which might operate behind them. The respect which Knightley has for Robert Martin, and which he comes to entertain for Harriet, or Elizabeth's being unaffected by "the mere stateliness of money and rank" at Rosings, and stirred to contempt by the pretensions she encounters there, show them to be, in Jane Austen's eyes, mannered in the highest degree.

A formal mannerliness which however is unaccompanied by kindness takes on the appearance of monstrosity wherever it occurs: whether it be the unsisterly correctness of Elizabeth Elliot, or the polite indifference of her cousin to the distress of his former friend Mrs. Smith consequent upon her loss of husband and affluence. The behaviour of the heroes and heroines alike in this connection seems to confirm Geoffrey Chaucer's dictum that "pitee renneth sone in gentil herte"[21]. One would expect it to be less with men, and perhaps least in the manliest of them all; but Frederick Wentworth provides some of the most notable instances. He does so when Mrs. Musgrove's regrets over her lost son interpose in the conversation at the Great House, as, despite a flicker of amusement at recollecting the midshipman he had been at pains to get rid of, he seats himself by her and talks "with so much sympathy and natural grace, as shewed the kindest consideration for all that was real and unabsurd in the parent's feelings". His action later during the walking party's return from Winthrop, in prevailing on the Crofts to give Anne a seat in their gig upon perceiving her tiredness, is "a proof of his own warm and amiable heart". While still blaming Anne for the past, and indifferent to her in the present, he yet "could not see her suffer, without the desire of giving her relief". But more eloquent of that heart's amiability are the words which burst from him at Louisa's apparent lifelessness after her fall from the Cobb at Lyme. Staggering against the wall for support, he exclaims "in the bitterest agony, 'Oh God! Her father and mother!'" This incident, according to Margaret Kennedy, shows that in Jane Austen's view, kindness and even tenderness is not the prerogative of women[22]. The evidence from Wentworth's character, certainly, is that it is in no wise unbecoming in a man.

Nor, for Jane Austen, is that spontaneity and element of impulsiveness which, though it can make mistakes, confirms a correspondence between outward and inward in a man's comportment. The same Captain Wentworth had unawares inflicted deep pain upon Anne Elliot after the first meeting at Uppercross, when he described her to another as being "so altered he should not have known you again". Ignoring the possibility that his words might be conveyed to her, he "had spoken as he felt". But it is precisely this naturalness of his, his "enthusiasm" as she terms it, which has endeared him to her: she prizes "the frank, the open-hearted, the eager character beyond all others". The charm it holds for her alone makes it possible for Wentworth to hope. Had she not experienced unease at the absence of "any burst of feeling, any warmth of indignation or delight" in Mr. Elliot, she might, chillingly, have been led by the "eligibilities and proprieties of the match" to accept him.

All these qualities, and many more, a man may have; but, put together, they will be unavailing without one further excellence: that of steadfastness. Here we come back to Lady Macbeth, as she strives finally in vain to urge on her faltering lord, and expresses a world of scorn in her accusation, "Infirm of purpose!"[23] Such wavering in a man's nature – above all in relation to the woman he loves – renders him unacceptable and contemptible in Jane Austen's estimation. A resoluteness – and a readiness as it were to take their lives into their hands in its service at the critical moment – is what qualifies her men as heroes, and enables them, often enough, to win their fair ones. Wentworth, finding himself suddenly released from Louisa, within five minutes has said to himself, "I will be in Bath on Wednesday". At the White Hart, hearing Ann's emotion-charged tones upon constancy in love, he seizes a pen and writes, "I must speak to you by such means as are within my reach" – and asks there and then for her hand, concluding, "A word, a look will be enough". Darcy, determinedly, twice makes moments to propose to Elizabeth by calling on her when she is alone at the Parsonage. On both occasions the attitude he meets there frustrates his intention; but he wastes no time when, at Longbourn, she has found courage enough to thank him for what he has done for them. Mr. Knightley, coming to Hartfield to console Emma after what he assumes has been Frank Churchill's betrayal, and finding to his astonishment that she is fancy-free, on "the immediate effect of what he heard" speaks for himself: his proposal is "the work of the moment". Henry Tilney, ordered by his father to acquiesce in the treatment he has meted out to Catherine, instead declares his intention to propose to her. Arrived at Fullerton, he invites her to walk with him the quarter of a mile to the Allen's house. "Some explanation on his father's account he had to give" during the course of it, Jane Austen remarks wryly; "but his first purpose was to explain himself, and before they reached Mr. Allen's grounds he had done it so well, that Catherine did not think it could ever be repeated too often".

To such a happy conclusion Henry Crawford has come near enough – when, while devoted to Fanny Price, he allows himself to be swayed from his overriding desire by one purely ephemeral. So, too, Willoughby, knowing himself united to Marianne by every tie of affection and mind, makes himself the willing victim of circumstance, incurring the world's and his own contempt. And Frank Churchill is of their kindred. It is the irresoluteness she has detected in his character which is largely responsible for distancing Emma from his influence. Heedless of the obligations of secrecy as of love, he can let a mere jocular whim, while the company at Hartfield is playing at alphabets, cause Jane Fairfax embarrassment and alarm, and jeopardize their situation; and his resentment at her declining to arouse suspicions by walking with him from Donwell all but drives them apart. He would have ruined both their lives, had not the death of the formidable Mrs. Churchill made their way clear for them. Mr. Knightley, with justification, terms Frank Churchill "the favourite of fortune". Margaret Kennedy, with the same justification, declares him to be "very nearly a villain"[24].

It is as if, in her estimation of men, and men in love, Jane Austen had taken as crowning truth words of her master Shakespeare upon creatures so sadly erratic and self-appeasing:

> O heaven! were man
> But constant, he were perfect: that one error
> Fills him with faults.²⁵

\* \* \*

The charge may be made against this assessment of Jane Austen's men that it gives undue prominence to Mary Bennet's commonplaces upon pride and vanity. But even greater opprobrium may be impending. For it cannot be brought to an end without a bold assertion: that, despite the limitations which literary convention subjected her to, and all that contemporary tastes and attitudes imposed on her as a woman, and whatever disqualification her own being a woman implies, Jane Austen understood men as well as she understood women. The novels, I would claim, show this to be so. And I must venture even further, though upon grounds more commonplace. The number of women who can say of the man in their life, "I can read him like a book" is, by common knowledge, legion. But the tally of men able with conviction to return the compliment will make a relatively modest showing. For, as Oscar Wilde defined the matter, "men can be analysed, women... merely adored"²⁶. I will therefore go so far as to declare that in all probability Jane Austen's understanding of men exceeded that of her women.

Is this an Aunt Sally by way of conclusion? Or treachery? Or heresy? Upon so grave an issue, I can only, as Mr. Bennet to his spouse, reply to the indignant questioner," I leave it to yourself to determine". But I am perfectly sure that, however much feelings may intensify and convictions clash, argument upon such a writer as Jane Austen will never degenerate into dispute: for, with this supreme creator of comedy, truth is at one with good-humour. So if there be matter here for contention, let that battle rage from which each combatant can only emerge victorious.

## ii

# *Persuasion*'s Unwritten Story

"Westgate Buildings!" said he; "and who is Miss Anne Elliot to be visiting in Westgate Buildings? – A Mrs. Smith. A widow Mrs. Smith, – and who was her husband? One of the five thousand Mr. Smiths whose names are to be met with every where… A poor widow, barely able to live, between thirty and forty – a mere Mrs. Smith, an every day Mrs. Smith, of all people and names in the world, to be the chosen friend of Miss Anne Elliot, and to be preferred by her, to her own family connexions among the nobility of England and Ireland! Mrs. Smith, such a name!" (157-8)

The expostulation of Sir Walter Elliot in response to his daughter's declining Lady Dalrymple's invitation in order to visit a former school friend in reduced circumstances. This demonstration of the full flow of his rhetorical and indeed intellectual powers does no more than confirm to the reader the first half of Admiral Croft's earlier observation, that "the baronet will never set the Thames on fire"; but the other half, that "there seems no harm in him", is disproved by the tirade's so wounding the feelings of the otherwise self-possessed Mrs. Clay as to make it impossible for her to stay in the room. In terms of the fortunes of its auditors, it is a far more potent pronouncement than immediately appears. Well considered, it might be found to constitute a turning point in the story.

Not that there is a great deal of substance in the remark; it would have been surprising if there were. True enough, when the author wishes to attribute the status of a nobody to one of her characters, Smith is the surname she seems to fall back upon – as with Emma Woodhouse's protégée Harriet, the mere parlour-boarder at Mrs. Goddard's school, and illegitimate daughter of a "respectable tradesman". But, the matter of status apart, the name itself demonstrably signifies little, if anything. In the course of the novel, Harriet displays such qualities of simplicity, good-nature and tenderness as can cause Emma on occasion to believe Harriet her superior, and capable of attaching men of wealth and social pretension. Roused by Mr. Knightley's attack on their friendship as an impropriety, she not only asserts that "such a girl as Harriet is exactly what every man delights in", but tells him, "Were you yourself ever to marry, she is the very woman for you" (64). Nor, as the world goes, does her opinion seem greatly to err. What reader of *Emma* would deny Harriet's natural and touching dignity towards the close, when she confides her hopes of Knightley's heart – or would at that point reject as a possibility what Emma, despite her every wish, cannot bring herself to do?

The conclusion must be – is it not part of the truth Jane Austen is presenting to us? – that, as it is with her Christian names, so with the surnames, they are in themselves no guide to the assessment of personality, or necessarily of social standing: that, in fact, the rose given another name, or placed within a different category, will smell as sweet. And of this there is corroboration in the other Smith in the novels: the very Mrs. Smith to whom Sir Walter Elliot without knowing her is moved to take such strong objection. Despite her being through poverty and misfortune resident in the unthinkable Westgate Buildings, she shows herself in manners, mind and disposition to be indisputably a lady, and even Anne's superior by right of seniority and knowledge of the world.

This, if a possible doubt – and a serious one – can first be laid to rest. It concerns the soundness or otherwise of her judgment in a prolonged declining to divulge her knowledge of Mr. Elliot's past selfish and cold-hearted demeanour to the friend she believes all but engaged to him in his new situation and persona. When the confidence is at last bestowed, there is amongst Anne's varied emotions so strong a puzzlement at its not having been forthcoming, and, more, at Mrs. Smith's having "seemed to recommend and praise" Mr. Elliot in the interim, that, well-mannered as she is, she cannot withhold an exclamation of surprise. Is she not justified? Can there be anything admirable in default upon so vital an issue, and whatever might lie behind it?

* * *

On the face of it, Mrs. Smith's behaviour is inconsistent. Instead of the needful communication, Anne has been offered a series of oblique queries and surmises all oddly indicating approval of the approaching marriage. She hopes and trusts her dear Miss Elliott "will be very happy". When might she speak of it as settled: "Next week?" Why should Miss Elliot be "cruel" enough to affect indifference to Mr. Elliot? Where would she "look for a more suitable match", or "expect a more gentlemanlike, agreeable man?" The change to incommunicativeness and silence that succeeds makes all the more shocking the vehemence of Mrs. Smith's denunciation when it bursts forth.

> "Mr. Elliot is a man without heart or conscience; a designing, wary, cold-blooded being, who thinks only of himself; who, for his own interest or ease, would be guilty of any cruelty, or any treachery, that could be perpetrated without risk of his general character…He is totally beyond the reach of any sentiment of justice or compassion. Oh! he is black at heart, hollow and black!" (199)

It should not escape us, however, that, no sooner are these accusations out of her mouth, than Mrs. Smith is begging her startled friend to "allow for an injured woman". In this recognition of her conduct having gone beyond decorous bounds, might we detect awareness that the position she is taking towards the person who has provoked it is likewise extreme? What, after all, are the offences she has taxed him with? We should do well to inquire, and consider whether they amount to what the poet might term "direct villainy".

There are a number of them. In his early years, Elliot had been guilty of a spendthrift style of living, and of an inclination also undeniable to escape from the trammelling constraints and expectations imposed by the accident of birth. His having found Sir Walter insufferable, insulting as this might seem to Anne Elliot, would elsewhere be deemed a sign of discernment and good taste. The desire to marry for money which subsequently motivated him, while naturally censurable, was one of those things which even Mrs. Smith admitted to be "too common" for outright condemnation, and which so discriminating a young woman as Elizabeth Bennet could view to be allowable in "A man in distressed circumstances", as Elliot was then by Mrs. Smith's account. The fact of his unkindness to his first wife, blemish though it may be, she is likewise from personal knowledge in a position to explain, and excuse. All these faults, while they show Mr. Elliot to be deserving of the title *homme moyen sensuel*, do not mark him down as a villain.

The monstrosity in his nature, if that is what it is, resides in his stern and unpitying refusal to come to the newly-widowed Mrs. Smith's aid, after the bankruptcy and death of the husband who had been his close friend. Estimable in any light such conduct cannot be; but in a certain light it could be seen as defensible. Now affluent, having, as Mrs. Smith puts it, "long had as much money as he could spend, nothing to wish for on the side of avarice or indulgence" (206), he has with the passing of years become intent upon the dignity destined for him in the future baronetcy. With entire propriety, therefore, he had proceeded to drop his former acquaintance upon her impoverishment and loss of social status: her becoming, so to speak, a mere Smith. In acting thus he had reverted to type and class: had "given her up", in the common phrase, with as little thought or compunction as Lady Bertram gave up the sister who had so "disobliged her family" as to bestow her affections upon a Lieutenant of Marines – or as Emma would have had to give up her dear Harriet if she had accepted Mr. Martin's letter of proposal.

Elliot's conduct had been deeply wounding and humiliating, deserving, perhaps, of a term like inhumanity; certainly in the estimation of Anne Elliot, face to face as she was now with grief and despair in her friend. But was she truly in any position to judge? Had she not, it might be asked, herself been guilty of inflicting real suffering, and upon much the same principle, in giving up her friend and lover, Frederick Wentworth, for the sake of "the independence which alone had been wanting"? And done so, in a daughter's more dependent situation, through conformity with the wisdom of that age, and of its spokesman in the figure of Lady Russell? The grief occasioned had not been his alone. Anne had borne a burden of sorrow long thereafter; but, at the time, she had "had to encounter all the additional pain of feelings, on his side, totally unconvinced and unbending, and of his feeling himself ill-used by so forced a relinquishment" (28). While still of course exercising fitting restraint, might he not in his exasperation have harboured the very supposition Mrs. Smith was to entertain of another, that Anne was a woman "without heart or conscience, a designing, wary, cold-blooded being who thinks only of herself"? What he did say, we are left to surmise; but to judge by what we know of his disposition, his parting comments will have been reasonably explicit; and, once having uttered them, he certainly showed no disposition to linger. When he reappears after a long interval, the affront still rankles in him.

So it is with Mrs. Smith, too; but she is sufficiently aware of her world, and has lived in it long enough, to know that, while Mr. Elliot's behaviour was reprehensible, he did not and could not exemplify the charge she has made against him. Her knowledge is Jane Austen's own. Readers and critics can be excused for sometimes forgetting, in the midst of being so well entertained, that in her novels she was not writing about novels, but about life: where, as her fanciful Catherine Morland was brought perforce to admit, it is not a question of persons either being "as spotless as an angel" or "having the disposition of a fiend", but of their partaking of "a general mixture of good and bad" (NA 200). In ordinary social intercourse, some may incur our dislike, a few perhaps justifiably our ire; but we should be unfortunate indeed to find ourselves confronted with a Montoni.

Through most of the fateful interview in her noisy parlour, however, Mr. Elliot was not Mrs. Smith's chief concern, though having been her first. The extremity of her need had made her resolve upon a renewed application, through Anne, to the man who had once spurned her appeal for help; but the presence of this very Miss Elliot was soon to impose upon her a problem far more critical and urgent: nothing less than that of making or marring the life's happiness of the friend she had rejoiced so unexpectedly to encounter. The engagement which she had gathered from all the indications to be about to take place, though apparently not yet a settled thing, was still very likely to happen; and she must now immediately decide whether, and by what right, she might take it upon herself to ensure that it never did.

In that ceremonious age, marriage was deemed not the product of romance, but a matter of family alliance. Within the bounds of her experience it would have been all but impossible for Mrs. Smith to have come upon a match of greater acceptability to the two immediately concerned, or to their family and acquaintances, who were from her certain information delighted at the prospect. All Anne's disavowals notwithstanding, the betrothal seemed near; in her features glowed the radiance of a young woman deeply in love. It betokened also the funds of future happiness which, despite the reservations Mrs. Smith entertained, might well be in store for the pair. For her merely to mention them would be a work of negation: of the destruction of possibility, with consequences unknown.

In its every detail, her subsequent conduct incurs no fault. First, dismissal of the subject of her previous friendship with Mr. Elliot: "It is a great time since we met", she tells Anne. Next comes the hesitation, and the inconsequential remarks often indicative of profound thought, to be followed by those inferences and refined delvings as to the state of Anne's emotions, legitimate in the circumstances, through which she hopes to arrive at a certainty. Then the composed responses to the rallying liveliness of Anne's inquiries, the less than polite short answers, and, finally, the muteness to which she is driven. But not before Anne, in her embarrassment at what was being asked of her, has made clear that her feelings relate to someone else, that "it is not Mr. Elliot that —"; and Mrs. Smith, in sensitive and mannered reaction, has instantly accepted her word, "and with all the semblance of seeing nothing beyond" (194-8).

Almost as soon, her decision has been made, and she is talking "in her natural tone of cordiality": asking pardon, confessing her previous uncertainty as to what to do, pleading the dislike any decent person feels "to be officious, to be giving bad impressions, making mischief" in the lives of others, and, at last, speaking without reserve her condemnation of the man by whom she has been wronged. The account is lengthy; by the time it is over her mood has changed to a considerate solemnity. The last we hear from her, drawn forth by Anne's wonderment at her first seeming commendation of Mr. Elliot, deserves not to be ignored.

> "My dear," was Mrs. Smith's reply, "there was nothing else to be done. I considered your marrying him as certain, though he might not yet have made the offer, and I could no more speak the truth of him, than if he had been your husband. My heart bled for you, as I talked of happiness. And yet, he is sensible, he is agreeable, and with such a woman as you, it was not absolutely hopeless. He was unkind to his first wife. They were wretched together. But she was too ignorant and giddy for respect, and he had never loved her. I was willing to hope that you must fare better." (211)

For Mrs. Smith to have come through so severe and agonising a test of friendship as this is nothing less than a triumph of good sense and good breeding. Where in the novels is there to be found a better example of sensitivity, discretion, principle, and kindness?

\*   \*   \*

None would deny that the surname of Smith, which Sir Walter finds so offensively plebeian, is undistinguished: but there is another in *Persuasion* which, if anything, is even more so. Not that it is borne by so many persons; but, in respect of the associations of the word, what can be commoner than Clay? which name Jane Austen accords to the widowed daughter of Sir Walter' steward, frequent visitor at Kellynch Hall, and long-term resident in Camden Place. From these particulars a somewhat unfortunate juxtaposition might be deduced. But the lady is a rung or two up the social ladder in her father's being a lawyer – a minor profession, at least, despite its provoking the merriment of Caroline Bingley and Mrs. Hurst at Netherfield Park, and the scorn of Emma Woodhouse for its representative in Highbury, the pert William Cox. In the novels' world, Mrs. Clay might be no more than on a par with Elizabeth Bennet's rather deplorable uncle Phillips: but she is also the equal of Elizabeth's first love and eventual brother-in-law, George Wickham, the possessor of manners more appealing than those of Mr. Darcy, and of social powers far more considerable.

In these latter respects, Mrs. Clay on her first appearance is as impressive. Quite at her ease in the rarefied atmosphere of Kellynch, she is as ready to promote her father's interests by extolling the virtues of a sailor tenant, as to contradict the baronet in mock remonstrance at his strictures upon the Navy, with her, "Nay, Sir Walter, this is being severe indeed. Have a little mercy on the poor men. We are not all born to be handsome". Clearly, a pronounced if not laudable ability is being displayed, in that this and her other challenges are at the same time instinct with flattery. Having gone through the list of occupations, with their blighting effects upon the practitioners, she turns to the situation of "those who are not obliged to follow any, who can live in a regular way, in the country, choosing their own hours, following their own pursuits, and living on their own property, without the torment of trying for more", the halcyon leisure of the privileged: and concludes with the splendid compliment, "it is only *their* lot, I say, to hold the blessings of health and a good appearance to the utmost". Could her words be other than music to the vain Sir Walter's ears?

A lively and spirited personality is before us. It does not give evidence of the wit and brilliancy of, say, a Mary Crawford, but shows itself possessed of intellect as powerful as hers. And also, in the processes of conversation, an elegance. If to a degree the speech is an indication of the person, then in the style of the words just quoted, or in her observation that "even in the quieter professions, there is a toil and labour of the mind, if not of the body, which seldom leaves a man's looks to the natural effect of time", rings evidence of Mrs. Clay's being someone worthy of note. But what greater proof can there be, than the fact of her having gained the friendship of the haughty Elizabeth Elliot, and suspicion of arousing the ardour of Sir Walter himself – who, in urging her to prolong her stay in his house, can so surprisingly yet deservedly pay tribute to her "fine mind" (20-1)?

This application was the very last thing his neighbour Lady Russell would have approved. Mrs. Clay's association with the Kellynch family was, for her, "an intimacy, which she wished to see interrupted", a friendship "quite out of place". Due allowance must be made for the "prejudices on the side of ancestry" which, Jane Austen informs us, could have the effect of narrowing her sympathies. Whether the estimate of Mrs. Clay as "a clever young woman, who understood the art of pleasing; the art of pleasing, at least, at Kellynch Hall" is that of Lady Russell or the author herself is impossible to determine; but in the sight of the former, the lady is "a very unequal, and in character she believed a very dangerous companion" for Elizabeth who ought to have been "nothing to her but the object of distant civility" (15-6).

However, in the scope of the novel as a whole, this judgment, or the thinking which leads to it, cannot be sound: for, eight years before, Lady Russell had made a similar objection, for pretty much the same reasons, to the man Anne Elliott finally marries. Wentworth she had seen as an unequal companion in his being entirely lacking in wealth; and the very self-confidence through which he was thereafter to amass a fortune "added a dangerous character to himself". In short, "She deprecated the connexion in every light", and prevailed on Anne to end it (27). Wrong as she has proved about him, can she now be right about Mrs. Clay?

Nevertheless, Lady Russell's opinion is one Anne shares and maintains, unyieldingly, to the last. She feels "quite as keenly" as the older woman the inappropriateness of the plan for Mrs. Clay to accompany her father and sister to Bath, especially in view of Sir

Walter's susceptibility, and is moved by the threat to his family to warn Elizabeth of it; and her immediate concern upon coming to Bath is to ascertain whether he was by now in love with Mrs. Clay. She is naturally more knowledgeable than Lady Russell, and also more observant. She well knew her father's propensity "to be constantly making severe remarks" in her absence upon Mrs. Clay's freckles and projecting tooth and clumsy wrist: but the charm of her being "decidedly altogether well-looking" Anne still does not underestimate. And she has sensed an attribute far more potent, in her possessing "in an acute mind, and assiduous pleasing manners, infinitely more dangerous attractions than any merely personal might have been" (34). Intellectually and socially, Mrs. Clay is a gifted being – a fact which must strongly influence the attitude Anne adopts towards her.

Is there a fear in Anne Elliot of being put in the shade? In a sense, this had already happened, long before Mrs. Clay's advent; and long ago, also, she had "become hardened" to the state. For temperamental and other reasons, Anne was odd man out in that family – was "nobody with either father or sister: her word had no weight; her convenience was always to give way" (5). She is a steady, serious character, in manner gentle and self-effacing; it is typical of her that, much as she is minded to reply upon her father's reproof at her visits in Westgate Buildings, she says nothing.

Whenever she speaks at length, it appears that she does so by effort. She is happier and more herself in making what is best described as minimal comment; though it is not insignificant that a quiet remark from her can be unusually forceful. In contrast to Mrs. Clay's long speeches in defence of the Navy, Anne's mild observation that they have "at least an equal claim with any other set of men" not only commands respect, but serves to direct the conversation (19). In the very different setting of the windy Cobb after Louisa's fall, when the party are transfixed with horror, Anne's words, again sparing, are of instant effect, for they proceed from a clear and resolute understanding. "A surgeon!" precipitates action: "Captain Benwick, would it not be better for Captain Benwick?" a change of plan (110). When, at the

Harville's, she is obliged to affirm her willingness to stay and look after Louisa, it is done as briefly as courtesy will permit. Rather than springing from any sense of inadequacy, this reserve in Anne Elliot seems the sign of a personal integrity and assurance.

The same may be said concerning that helpfulness of disposition which is as constant in her as it is unaffected. It is not just out of duty, but evidently with pleasure that she has industriously made catalogues of the books and pictures at Kellynch, sorted out the plants to be taken or left, and gone to almost every house in the parish as a take-leave. Again, her instinct when the newly-engaged Henrietta confides her anxieties about her husband's future is a readiness "to do good" by entering interestedly into the subject, acquiescing in Henrietta's sentiments and wishes, and adding kindly encouragement of her own. And, upon her coming to stay at Kellynch Lodge, and hearing Lady Russell discoursing about the Kellynch family's concerns when her own thoughts were engrossed by the people at Lyme, and the friendship of the Harvilles and Captain Benwick, she consciously makes the exertion which courtesy demands, to be able "to meet Lady Russell with any thing like the appearance of equal solicitude, on topics which had by nature the first claim on her" (124). All this is simple good manners, of course, but it is also genuine good will: the two are not very much dissimilar.

In the ordinary course of events, Anne Elliot's reactions always tend to be natural and right, often even laudable. Upon her visiting the Crofts at Kellynch after they have taken possession, no thought of her own family's loss afflicts her: she "could but in conscience feel, that they were gone who deserved not to stay" (125). The Admiral's wayward and sometimes brusque manners do not obscure for her that "goodness of heart" in which she takes such delight; though his perplexity at the number of mirrors in her father's room, and their declaring him "a rather dressy man for his time of life", leaves her, while amused in spite of herself, apprehensively "at a loss for an answer". The barely suppressed grief of Captain Harville, as he speaks of the sister so recently lost, is met with her suggestion, comforting though it be commonplace, "but in time, perhaps – we know what time does in every case of affliction" (108). By the thought, when first she is in Westgate Buildings, of the instances of selflessness and fortitude in human nature at its noblest which must pass before those who nurse the sick, Anne is moved; and in the crippled Mrs. Smith's cheerfulness, her power of transforming an evil into good, she reverently finds "the choicest gift of Heaven".

Such sentiments, while not novel, have nothing of the pretentious about them, but are entirely just. And the same holds true of her responses in encounters with the opposite sex: while they are properly modest, there is nothing missish about them. Finding herself being very directly complimented by Mr. Elliot during the interval of the concert, she reacts blushingly with an attempt to change the conversation: "'For shame, for shame! – this is too much of flattery. I forget what we are to have next,' turning to the bill" (187). But she will restrain neither her pleasure nor her inquiries at Charles Musgrove's news of Captain Benwick's admiring her exceedingly, despite Mary's graceless disparagement of the idea; and from that time her head is full of the thought of meeting or seeing him again. And why not?

*   *   *

What, however, distinguishes Anne's behaviour from that of a Catherine Morland in her inexperience, and of an Elizabeth Bennet in her capacity to be misled by her spirits, is the implicit conformity to standards which never fails her: standards of decorum, needless to say, and also of morality. The briefest of chance meetings with a stranger at a seaside inn reveal him, "by the readiness and propriety of his apologies" (104), to be a befitting object for her approval and interest. But the excellent manners of this person prove insufficient seriously to recommend him. In themselves they are pleasing to her, as they are commendable by the precepts of her day; but beyond them, she cannot be satisfied that she really knows his character. Hints of bad habits, of a past carelessness on serious matters, have arisen from further acquaintance with him; and though in mature years he might have come to think differently, what, she asks herself, were now his sentiments – and "How could it ever be ascertained that his mind was truly cleansed?" (161)

We are dealing here with an engaging severity, not unlike that sometimes displayed by Fanny Price, but wider-ranging and better informed: with a conceptual kind of thinking, in fact, of sufficient depth to be able, when occasion demands, to capture the essence of that age's outlook, and state it with admirable conciseness. Consider the advice she gives to young Captain Benwick, impassioned as he allows himself to become, that evening at the Harville's, under the influence of a broken heart and the tenderest outpourings of Scott and Byron: that she considers it poetry's misfortune "to be seldom safely enjoyed by those who enjoy it completely", and that "the strong feelings which alone could estimate it truly, were the very feelings which ought to taste it but sparingly". Is it not the voice of the eighteenth century itself that we are hearing in her dictum – or in the recommendation that Benwick apply himself instead to the study of works of morality and memoirs "calculated to arouse and fortify the mind by the highest precepts, and the strongest of moral and religious endurances" (100)? Unlike Fanny Price, whose reflections, devout traditionalist though she is, show her as standing almost on the brink of romanticism, Anne Elliot reveals herself in these speeches to be a thoroughgoing conventionalist.

And she is declared so by another and yet more formidable constituent of her nature – whose presence there is most pronounced upon occasions when it might be expected to be least in evidence. One comes as she and Wentworth, restored to each other at last, are pacing the quiet and retired gravel-walk in Bath, oblivious of the bustling life around them, explaining to each other through those precious moments their past actions and feelings. Wentworth is eloquent upon his despair during the concert at seeing her in the company of the same Lady Russell who had before persuaded her to reject him. Anne is genuinely surprised that he should have so misjudged. Previously, she had yielded to persuasion on the side of safety, as was her duty; but could he not have seen that in Bath she was not duty-bound; indeed, that in marrying a man "indifferent" to her she would have violated duty through the risk she was taking? Quite how Wentworth was to recognise and be sure of this indifference she does not explain, and probably would be unable to say: but what is transparently clear to her – and, she feels, ought to be as obvious to him – is duty as a moving principle where she is concerned. Diplomatically enough, Wentworth answers, "Perhaps I ought to have reasoned thus, but I could not" (245). We can only sympathise.

Anne Elliott appears to be on remarkably good terms with the "Stern daughter of the voice of God"; so much so, that she dedicates the ensuing opportunity of tender communication to a further exposition. It is after the drawing rooms at Camden Place have been lighted up, the company at Miss Elliot's card party assembled, and the two have stolen away in pretended admiration of a display of greenhouse plants. She has been trying, she tells Wentworth, to judge her own action in obeying Lady Russell – "whom", she confides, "you will love better than you do now". And she had been right to do so, despite the eight and a half years of separation, since otherwise, "I should have suffered in my conscience". And, as emphatically, she concludes:

> "I have now, as far as such a sentiment is allowable in human nature, nothing to reproach myself with; and if I mistake not, a strong sense of duty is no bad part of a woman's portion." (246)

Wentworth replies only by referring to the point of his future relationship with Lady Russell: the disquisition itself is studiously, and one may think advisedly, ignored. If Anne expected concurrence with the final remark, or with the incipient self-congratulation which had gone before, none was to be forthcoming. One is possibly entitled to infer from Wentworth's silence, as well as some suppressed alarm, the disinclination any lover would feel to encourage the beloved in such flights into the moralistic sublime. The notion that she would have suffered greater disquiet in being with him than the pain she had endured in being without him is not one likely to recommend itself to the hero, whatever satisfaction it might afford the heroine.

Perhaps our best resort for adjudging this idiosyncrasy in Anne Elliot is to Jane Austen herself, who, in mentioning *Persuasion* to her niece Fanny Knight, wrote, "You will not like it, so you need not be impatient. You may *perhaps* like the Heroine, as she is almost too good for me"[27]. Such a confession from such a source is not do be disregarded. It gains credence from the apt comment of her biographer Elizabeth Jenkins, that, after her initial blunder in breaking off her engagement with the man she truly loved, Anne "never makes a single error in morality, judgement or taste"; but she points out that her character nonetheless remains neither priggish nor unreal, finding the reason to lie in her clear-sightedness as to her family's failings, and the tremulous experience of emotion's depths and heights, which combine to "keep her altogether vulnerable and human"[28].

Anne's sensitivity to the "thousand natural shocks" life has for us does to an extent moderate, or rather reconcile us to, the goodness in question. But there is a further ingredient of her personality, no less human and humbling, which may however properly lead us to speculate whether the "goodness" Jane Austen comes near to reprehending in Anne Elliot is not to be regarded as somewhat more social than moral, though pertaining to both sorts of virtues: as being rather a correctness, in keeping with the age's delineations, as to what was ideal and so appropriate for admiration and imitation in a young woman, while yet with respect to the former incurring some tincture of that society's austerities.

At the risk of slight injustice to Anne, the suggestion can be made that it might be detected in a wholly inconsequential remark of hers to Mrs. Smith, who had asked whether she had noticed the woman who opened the door to her the previous day. Anne's reply is, "No. Was it Mrs. Speed, as usual, or the maid? I observed no one in particular" (197). The omission had been innocent: it is not incumbent upon, or in the habit of, young ladies like herself to pay any special attention to servants. Nor to the lower orders in general. For this reason, the pleasure which Mrs. Smith confesses she has derived from listening to Nurse Rooke strikes Anne as somewhat singular; but, "far from wishing to cavil at" it she responds with the thought that, "Women of that class have great opportunity, and if they are intelligent may be worth listening to" (155). Harmless truism though this be, it is at the same time in the nature of a concession – and one from which it may be safely conjectured that Anne has done little listening of that variety. These are incidental touches, and in themselves carry little weight; but they are germane to the far more definite comment later on in the session, provoked by Mrs. Smith's inability, during the years of her early acquaintance with Mr. Elliot, to see much wrong in his marrying for money, when this was so common a preoccupation amongst the young men they then knew. "But was she not a very low woman?" Anne asks. There is an incredulity and near expostulation in the remark, which imparts a note of finality. It is to be noticed that Mrs. Smith wholly accords with the sentiment.

In this attitude, both are being correct. Even for the rich and seemingly less fastidious Emma Woodhouse, the evident "indifference to a confusion of rank" in Frank Churchill's recommending a fortnightly ball at the Crown Inn, despite the objection urged upon him of "the want of proper families" in the neighbourhood, "bordered upon inelegance of mind" unacceptable in someone of his station (E 198). Is Anne Elliot to be blamed for sharing views so universally held?

That she has them is certain; but in a curious way she is made to profess a discrepant freedom with regard to rank at variance with the otherwise instinctive and conventional position she takes. When Mr. Elliot seeks to persuade her of the importance of their accepting Lady Dalrymple's preparedness to welcome them, and enjoying "all the advantages of the connexion as far as possible", she makes the almost heretical assertion, in intimating, "I suppose (smiling) I have more pride than any of you", that they have been too solicitous in getting the relationship acknowledged, and that she is and must remain "too proud to enjoy a welcome which depends so entirely upon place" (150). Her idea of good company she had already informed him to be that of "clever, well-informed people, who have a great deal of conversation"; and she does, to do her justice, in general show an impatience with society's externalities, like "the usual style of give-and-take invitations, and dinners of formality and display", and the tedious social gatherings which were "but a mixture of those who had never met before, and those who met too often" (245). Not that this tendency, errant though it be, will lead her too far astray. The prospect of becoming the next Lady Elliot through marriage with the heir presumptive, when first put before her by her friend Lady Russell, obliges Anne to turn and walk aside and pretend employment in the attempt to repress the feelings it creates: "For a few moments her imagination and her heart were bewitched" (160). It is realisation of the incapacity of the man in the affair to exercise bewitchment upon her that causes the dream to disperse; rank itself, and properly so, is under no such disqualification.

The effect of this irregularity – or inconsistency, as it might be supposed – in Anne's character is to make her appear to rise above, and so to obscure, her more ordinary attitude to the matter of rank and class. Jane Austen endows her with, as it were, a refreshing incorrectness which, in its humanity, is safe from criticism and beyond reproach, but which yet does not have sufficient hold to divide her from her more normal and conformable self. Thus is fulfilled a need in the heroine, and manifestly in the author, that Anne's condition of being "almost too good" do not develop into excess: that, though granted such impressive endowment of heroic charm, she will remain

> A creature not too bright or good
> For human nature's daily food –

particularly, as regards the social attitudes she was born to.

Thus, for all that it is undoubted and abundant in Anne Elliot, her good will may not extend to Mrs. Clay. Instead, there is a sophisticated watchfulness that is quick to detect a fault, to fathom the pretences she is often put to in her attentions to the family which has so condescendingly welcomed her into their midst. She is only a visitor when we first find her with them, the reason being – as Anne is aware of it – that her father Mr. Shepherd had driven her over, "nothing being of so much use to Mrs. Clay's health as a drive to Kellynch" (18). In the eagerness of her enumerating the depredations upon men's health and looks of professional practice, we are informed – again, it seems, in terms of Anne's recognition – that "she stopt a moment to consider what might do for the clergyman" (20). These contrivances, if they are at all culpable, are trifling; but that they are being viewed with suspicion, or scorn, cannot be denied. Such perceptions in Anne are illustrative of a dislike, or even an antagonism, that is unrelieved to the novel's end. Even the "pleasant and smiling" greeting she receives from Mrs. Clay upon her coming to Bath is contemptuously regarded: "Anne had always thought she would pretend what was proper on her arrival" (137).

Without doubt, it is the danger she constitutes to her own and her sister's prospects which gives rise to this critical spirit; but the reality of the hurt is plain. Anne's early encounters with Mrs. Clay in Camden Place are diversified by Mr. Elliot's frequent visits; and what makes Anne ready to overlook his lenient censure of the notion of good society she puts to him is the intimated disapproval of the lady they both see as outside its bounds: "she was pleased with him for not liking Mrs. Clay; and her conscience admitted that his wishing to promote her father's getting great acquaintance, was more than excusable in the view of defeating her" (151). The being afterwards put on her guard against him by Mrs. Smith's revelation plunges her therefore into a rather diverting state of exasperation.

> It was bad enough that Mrs. Clay should be always before her; but that a deeper hypocrite should be added to their party, seemed the destruction of every thing like peace and comfort. (215)

To be set between a Scylla and a Charybdis in the confines of a drawing room is a fate no one would envy.

Is it pure alarm at "the results the most severe to his family" that would follow from her father's marrying Mrs. Clay which causes Anne to warn the sister "who in the event of such a reverse would be so much more pitied than herself"? Or is there an admixture of fear of the disgrace which Mrs. Clay's "low" condition would bring upon them all? There is nothing about the latter possibility in what she says to Elizabeth; but it is almost entirely in terms of rank that she is answered, inheritance as such being relegated almost to an afterthought. "Mrs. Clay", Elizabeth tells her with warmth, "never forgets who she is"; more strongly than most people, "she reprobates all inequality of condition and rank"; and her sentiments upon marriage are in this respect "particularly nice" (35). The substance of the matter, though unstated in Anne's approach, is asserted by Elizabeth, and understood by both, to be the formidable barrier of social decorum which they know to exist, and behind which, presumably, they should feel themselves secure.

Upon that bulwark, the visit Anne was to make to Mrs. Smith is nothing less than a formal assault: clear defiance of established custom. And not without due deliberation and caution is it undertaken. From the personal viewpoint, Anne was reasonably confident of not being grossly in error. Apart from intervening misfortunes since they had last seen each other, Mrs. Smith had strong claims upon her in her present crippled state, and in that past kindness when Anne had returned to school grieving over her mother's death, "which had considerably lessened her misery, and could never be remembered with indifference" (152). These considerations, however, were in themselves not enough: for an affair of such moment, it was needful to have recourse to an elder's experience and principle, and Lady Russell was applied to. Her judgment was favourable: Anne's youthful friendship, the then Miss Hamilton's comfortable circumstances and her subsequently becoming the wife of a man of fortune, as well as charitable concern for an invalid, sufficiently militated against her present penniless condition for Anne to renew acquaintance with her. But Lady Russell's preparedness to convey her "as near to Mrs. Smith's lodgings in Westgate Buildings as she chose to be taken" betokens the equivocal nature of the proceeding in the minds of both ladies (153). A stern critic – and what is more, a fair and impartial one – might see in it an apprehension lest the coach and its owner should be so sullied by that proximity as to be in need of the month's ablution which Elizabeth irreverently imagined Mr. Darcy would resort to, "in order that he might be cleansed from the impurities of Gracechurch Street were he once to enter it" (PP 141).

But this time Lady Russell's judgment had been sound. Once the awkwardness and emotion of the first moments have faded, Mrs. Smith is, for Anne, as much still the lady of her remembrance, as Mr. Elliot the gentleman when she again sets eyes on him. Yet she has not been without trepidation as to what change intervening years and events might have brought about in her erstwhile friend. Happily, we are informed, as the meeting progressed, Anne finds in Mrs. Smith "the good sense and agreeable manners which she had almost ventured to depend on" (153). The intimation of verb and adverb conjoined surely is testimony to the existence in Anne Elliot of apprehensions concerning the venture she was engaged upon, not so very far removed from Sir Walter's own. But swiftly they have been done away. It cannot be said at this point that she has crossed the Rubicon of social decorum: but she is now at least safely over one of its lesser tributaries.

For what would have been her feelings if Sir Walter had recklessly launched himself across this fateful waterway with regard to Mrs. Clay, and grandly set foot upon the opposite bank? Would they not have amounted to such dismay as afflicted Emma Woodhouse at the thought of Mr. Knightley married to Harriet Smith?

> Such an elevation on her side! Such a debasement on his! – It was horrible to Emma to think how it must sink him in the general opinion, to foresee the smiles, the sneers, the merriment it would prompt at his expense – the mortification and disdain of his brother, the thousand inconveniences to himself. (413)

For any self-respecting gentleman such things would be sufficiently daunting. But for an individual as considerate of his dignity as Sir Walter Elliot, they would assume tragic proportions.

But what of the subject of "elevation", which also exercises Miss Woodhouse's mind? Who, let the question be asked, being in social terms a nobody, is to be seen in the novels as achieving acceptability and bliss? Addressing it, we find ourselves embarked upon a rather barren quest. There are, for a start, very few persons so identifiable.

\* \* \*

Edmund Bertram, humble as his ambitions and his finances are, is not a candidate: the younger son of a baronet, with "a very good living" kept for him thereabouts, as Miss Crawford has not failed to notice, cannot be so described. Nor can the well-born Edward Ferrars, who, after rejecting the choice of a Parliamentary or military career, finds himself arbitrarily disinherited, but is thereafter moderately redeemed through the unexpected gift of a living. A similar calamity had befallen Elinor and Marianne Dashwood, heiresses of a wealthy old country family unfairly cut out through a trick of senility in their grandfather; but by the end they both manage to do quite reasonably well, their establishments, while far from equal in affluence, being fortunately within thirty miles of each other.

Charles Hayter, though, is at first sight a different case, for his family were not people of any consequence. "And, pray, who is Charles Hayter?" Mary Musgrove asks. "Nothing but a country curate. A most improper match for Miss Musgrove, of Uppercross". But Mary is being rather too severe, as her husband points out to her. It would, he admits, "not be a *great* match for Henrietta"; but Mary is overlooking the fact that Charles Hayter has "a very fair chance, through the Spicers, of getting something from the Bishop" in due course, and that, elder son as he is, upon the death of his father "he steps into very pretty property" in the estate at Winthrop and the farm near Taunton. And "with that property", he concludes, "he will never be a contemptible man.

Good, freehold property" (76). However much this assurance may be unwelcome to Mary, her cousin Charles is unlikely to be despised by anyone other than herself.

Nor is his being a mere curate a hindrance. The clergy in that age had the mild distinction of being regarded as a class of sub-gentry, and tolerated as such, so long of course as they did not give themselves unbecoming airs – or otherwise, in the decorous words of Mr. Collins, "provided that a proper humility is at the same time maintained" (PP 97). Catherine Morland by this same standard deserves recognition. True, she is only a clergyman's daughter; but her father is the possessor not only of two livings, but of landed property which is to be his eldest son's future inheritance; and Catherine's dowry of three thousand pounds, while not great, is respectable.

Catherine's portion is three times the amount of Elizabeth Bennet's, however; and this sober truth brings into sharp question the matter of her status. Mrs. Bennet being left out of the reckoning, Elizabeth has the indubitable claim of being a gentleman's daughter. But since her father's estate of two thousand per annum is entailed from the female line, she is in practical terms all but dowerless: a consideration which, as Mr. Collins hatefully but correctly advises her, will "in all likelihood undo the effects of your loveliness and amiable qualifications", and make it "by no means certain that another offer of marriage may ever be made you" (PP 108). The inferiority of her social position not only calls forth Lady Catherine de Bourgh's unmitigated horror, but creates those "scruples" and provokes those "struggles" in Mr. Darcy so clearly unconsonant with his declaration of love, despite his guileless insistence upon their being "natural and just" in a man of his eminence. Neither they nor the reflection they constitute finally prevent her becoming mistress of Pemberley, but that development is a notable elevation; and her claim to social distinction, personable in every other respect though she is, has been only marginally admissible.

Whether it is as strong as that of *Sensibility*'s Mrs. Jennings is not easily determined. Mrs. Jennings never can have been, as Elizabeth is even in the eyes of Lady Catherine, "a very genteel, pretty kind of girl":

pretty or not, she was and remains incurably vulgar. We learn from John Dashwood that, as we might have guessed, she is "the widow of a man who got all his money in a low way"; but to this material detail must be added Elinor's serious caution to her mother, that "she is not a woman whose society can afford us pleasure, or whose protection will give us consequence" (SS 156). Yet in both respects, Miss Dashwood proves to be mistaken. Since her husband's death, Mrs. Jennings has taken to spending every winter "in a house in one of the streets near Portman Square", which, with her style of living, indicates "an exceedingly good income"; and, of more importance, her decency and warmth of heart so affect Elinor as to promote a highly unlikely but very firm friendship between them. Ill-bred, in her son-in-law's forthright and uncalled-for estimation, and Elinor's unspoken one, Mrs. Jennings may be; but, all things considered, her obvious wealth, and the irrefutable facts that one of her daughters is a Lady Middleton, and the other the wife of a Member of Parliament, will procure for her the complaisance of those she comes in contact with.

Quite who Mr. Smith was, who at his death left his affairs in such confusion, and his wife unprovided for, we are not to learn. His easiness of temper and "not strong understanding" had, as Anne Elliot gathers, between them kept him from retaining his fortune; yet that it had been considerable is evident from his widow's title to property in the West Indies, long "under a sort of sequestration for the payment of its own encumbrances", which Captain Wentworth finally recovers for her. The ensuing "improvement of income", together with some return of health, will, as well as creating in her "a spring of felicity", ensure the justification of any essay on Mrs. Smith's part to resume her former social standing – and discontinuance, it need not be said, of her residence in Westgate Buildings (252).

No such happiness does Willoughby gain or merit. For the wife who has freed him from his "dread of poverty" and conviction of "the necessity of riches", he comes to have unmeasured contempt. The fierce determination in one living above his income to make his fortune by marriage is understandable, though scarcely pardonable by the young woman he has jilted. Success of a kind he attains; bliss most emphatically he does not. But in all his actions, good and bad alike, he is seen to exemplify the manner and style of a gentleman. So also is the cultured Henry Crawford, more fortunate in that money-making need not be one of his preoccupations. With his captivating sister, he is at the centre of happenings at Mansfield Park. Their becoming involved in scandal and failure is the outcome of faults of character, and not related to their assured position in society.

Life, of course, will always have its casualties, even amongst the privileged and advantaged. Within the ranks of Jane Austen's commoners, however, it is a matter of adversity and mischance almost unrelieved. Which of them is not at the end, by social definition, a casualty: can be said to have come to good, to have progressed into status, and the dignified pleasures and eligibilities consequent upon it? Alas, it is not the artless Harriet Smith, who is finally hustled away and finds her proper place as the wife of Farmer Martin – to Emma's infinite relief, and with the dubious distinction of having been in love with three different men in a single year. The ultimate fates of the underbred John and Isabella Thorpe are not vouchsafed to us; but we may be confident that they are of as small concern to ourselves as to the novelist, and will have nothing at all prepossessing about them.

If it were only for the extensive role he plays, George Wickham would appear more fortunately destined. But his have been also the not insignificant benefits of being brought up at Pemberley, educated at Cambridge and intended for the Church; and in manners and address he is in no way inferior to Pemberley's present owner. His being the son of the late Mr. Darcy's steward is no more disabling to the reader than it is to Elizabeth Bennet when Caroline Bingley laughingly apprises her of it. Nor indeed is it a factor in the estimation of most persons the novel introduces us to, not excluding that of Fitzwilliam Darcy himself, if we accept his explanations. Yet by the end, Wickham is revealed as a liar, slanderer, philanderer and gamester: in the author's words, "one of the most worthless young men in Great Britain" (PP 308).

In descent, Mrs. Clay is Wickham's equal; and her deservings and final repute might seem to be almost a reflection of his own. For her course through events is aided by flattery and artifice, she evokes no good opinion, and contrives eventually to shock and mortify Sir Walter and Elizabeth, having failed in her intention to become the wife of the one, and stepmother of the other. What is to lie beyond for her is outside the novel's scope. We last hear of her as being established under Mr. Elliot's protection in London, there abandoned to the unsavoury endeavour of "wheedling and caressing" him into making her the next Lady Elliot. Succeed she may; but the inference through all we have seen of her association with the people of the novel, and particularly that person who is its heroine, is that she does not deserve to.

A distinct success, though one similarly unbeseeming, may be thought to have occurred in Lucy Steele's securing the witless Robert Ferrars as her husband. Certain it is that she gains, with him, both fortune and favour with her mother-in-law and her friends the Dashwoods. But in terms of the ensuing relationships, domestic and other, Lucy's victory is rather to be viewed as of the Pyrrhic sort, and the marriage itself as little other than merited penalty.

\* \* \*

Upon a mere two, perhaps three, persons who are nobodies can good fortune and approval by all the standards of Jane Austen's novels be seen to descend. These instances share a vital common element; and in one only is it not obvious.

Fanny Price, at the age of ten transplanted to Mansfield Park, appears to bear the brunt of a social system's severity. Uppermost in her uncle Sir Thomas Bertram's mind is "the distinction proper to be made" between the newcomer and his own daughters as they grow up, the line of conduct which will always impress her lack of claim upon her. So little have her interests been regarded, seemingly, that when she has reached her eighteenth year it is unclear to the Bertrams, and anyone of inquiring disposition, whether or not she is "out"; and she herself has never presumed to consider the subject.

At Mansfield Park there are a number of circumstances helpful to Fanny. She has had at her disposal all the appurtenances of dignified living which a great household can bestow – an immense boon, in comparison with the meagre conditions Emma Watson must compromise with. The behaviour of Maria and Julia Bertram can only confirm Fanny's innate shyness; but upon their departure from Mansfield she is left "the only young woman in the drawing-room", her consequence at home and at the Parsonage increasing to the extent of her having, at the latter, to fulfil the demands of being the principal lady in company. In the resolve constantly to keep before her the fact of her obscurity, her aunt is nothing less than an affliction; but relief comes from Sir Thomas's growing realisation that blood is thicker than water. For, though a commoner, Fanny is a well-connected one – a condition the author herself was not unfamiliar with. Her uncle begins at length to feel proud of his humble relation. He is not under Mrs. Norris's illusion that her beauty is attributable to her upbringing at Mansfield; however, "he was pleased with himself for having supplied everything else – education and manners she owed to him" (276). His protégée differs notably from Harriet Smith in being an excellent recipient of benefits: she possesses that liveliness of mind which, as Anne Elliot so well appreciated, is the height of attraction in a handsome woman.

Yet these not inconsiderable advantages do not of themselves promote the happiness Fanny attains: it is her association with the Navy which is to bring her to distinction. But for midshipman Price's coming, Sir Thomas would never have realised the possibilities in his niece. He encounters in young Price "frank, unstudied, but feeling and respectful manners"; but the effect of their naturalness upon Fanny is a release and joyous flowering "which her uncle could not but observe with complacency". He is moved repeatedly to call upon its occasioner to recount his experiences at sea (233-4), and the qualities manifest in them gain him Sir Thomas's esteem.

Thus, when William asks his uncle a question he cannot answer – "Is not Fanny a very good dancer, sir?" – the outcome, extraordinary for the demesne of sobriety Mansfield Park has been, is that approving determination to satisfy her brother's wish to see her dance which results in the festivity Sir Thomas decrees. To her initial horror, Fanny learns that "*she* was to lead the way and open the ball" as "the Queen of the evening". What in her humility she finds so overpowering is less the situation in the ballroom than the thought of the honour accorded her.

> She could hardly believe it. To be placed above so many elegant young women! The distinction was too great. It was treating her like her cousins! (275)

The ball at Mansfield scarcely marks the end of Fanny's trials and anxieties: but it establishes her in undisputed possession of those social privileges which will make possible her eventual achievement of a long despaired-of goal.

\* \* \*

Captain Frederick Wentworth is no scion of the Strafford family; and neither he nor his friend Captain Benwick is a gentleman in the strict term which Sir Walter withholds from Wentworth's clergyman brother, Edward. Not surprising are the strong grounds of objection the baronet must entertain towards the Navy: it is an institution by which all proper considerations of social decorum are disregarded, and anomalies of nefarious kind perpetrated. It is a means, he declares, "of bringing persons of obscure birth into undue distinction, and raising men to honours which their fathers and forefathers never dreamt of" – and men, to boot, who have been "all knocked about, and exposed to every climate, and every weather, until they are not fit to be seen" (201). From the latter charge, Wentworth is providentially spared; and as to the former, he may "hug himself". For Jane Austen, the Navy is the realm where the artificialities of her society are blown asunder and scattered, where true merit is revealed: the proving ground of courage, worth, and, yes, nobility. It is a small world in itself – but yet a world apart, removed in concept, as literally by distance, from the outlook and standards of the great and assured social order beneath whose dominance her own life was played out, and to whose enabling impositions she, with all those whom she knew, must ever yield.

*   *   *

In his *Memoir*, written in the year 1870, James Edward Austen-Leigh suggested that the reason for his aunt's laying aside *The Watsons* was that she had

> become aware of the evil of having placed her heroine too low, in such a position of poverty and obscurity as, though not necessarily connected with vulgarity, has a sad tendency to degenerate into it; and therefore, like a singer who has begun on too low a note, she discontinued the strain.[29]

The thought comes to us from an epoch much closer to Jane Austen's than ours, and by the hand of a nephew who might with delicacy be presenting as a surmise of his own, intimations from acquaintance with the writer herself. It is therefore deserving of attention.

In citing these words, however, Elizabeth Jenkins admits herself unimpressed by them. "One cannot feel that this reason is a convincing one", she comments, "if only because Emma Watson is shown to such triumphant advantage in the poverty and obscurity of her home"[30]. But, as the evidence of the novels taken together, and particularly of *Persuasion*, may lead us to conjecture, might it not be precisely because of this achievement in Emma Watson, so at variance with the assumptions and mood of those times, that Jane Austen found herself obliged to leave the work unfinished? That, despite all her insights and promptings as to the meretriciousness of "place", and the primacy of human worth, it was not in her nature to become a *bucinator novi temporis*, the herald of change to her contemporaries and her own intimates: to venture into territory untrodden by the polite authors of her day, or admit even to herself such a daunting possibility?

For this same cause (if we are at liberty to apply the phrase she used of herself as an historian) she makes her Anne Elliot resolutely "partial and prejudiced" – not to say "ignorant" – in her treatment of Mrs. Clay. Though never approaching the directness of Edmund Bertram in declaring a commoner's being on equal terms "an evil", Anne is at one with him, and with the restored Emma Woodhouse, in the simple practice of looking down upon those beneath them: in an implicit belief that it is a propensity beyond question, itself a rightness, and, in the social context, a modest but undeniable virtue. This tenet Emma has painfully to learn after her escapade with Harriet Smith; but Anne Elliot, as the very pattern of the ladylike – of feminine "goodness", as the age understood, and Jane Austen acknowledged, it – is incapable of a lapse of the sort.

In the character of Emma Woodhouse, and that of Emma Watson, and in the fortunes of such as Harriet Smith and Penelope Clay, we may see the externalisation of a conflict deep in the author's being: a contention between an instinctive revolt against the pretensions and oppressiveness of "place", and a compulsive adherence to it as the basis of decorum, agreeableness and elegance – in other words, of such goodness in the wide sense as human society is able to afford. And since, for her, these opposites must remain always locked in combat, so their struggle can find vigorous expression, but not resolution, in the novels' world. The presence of a Mrs. Clay can but prompt in Jane Austen the certitude aroused in Hamlet by a Claudius enthroned in Denmark, that "It is not nor it cannot come to good" [31]. Like the usurper, Mrs. Clay can appear to her only as a threatening intruder into a previously settled milieu – as much so, perhaps, as was the social upstart Wickham beneath Caroline Bingley's contemptuous gaze.

\*     \*     \*

Thus it comes about that, despite her constant observation, Anne Elliot is poorly placed for a true judgment of Mrs. Clay. The latter's recognition of the knock on the door at ten o'clock being Mr. Elliot's gains her notice: but it might have told her more. Mrs. Clay's encouraging the notion of a liking in Mr. Elliot for Elizabeth is picked up through the look the women exchange when the frequency of his visits is under discussion; nor does it elude Anne that Mrs. Clay should steal a glance at her sister and herself when being so very earnestly complimented by Sir Walter upon her "fine mind". But what escapes her is at least as much as what does not – and more remarkably so. While Sir Walter is delivering his vilification of the proletarian Smiths, the fact that Mrs. Clay "thought it advisable to leave the room" is obvious to the rest of them; but Anne "left it to himself to recollect, that Mrs. Smith was not the only widow in Bath between thirty and forty, with little to live on, and no sirname of dignity". This awareness, evidently absent from the other two, is strongly present in her. But its not bringing her to realise the blow his aspersion must have constituted to Mrs. Clay's hopes of the baronet, and the acuteness of the resulting distress which will have accompanied her departure, is more than strange.

It might be held that literary necessity has demanded her imperception here: that an Anne Elliot at this early stage perceiving Mrs. Clay's purpose to have been thwarted, or as unlikely to succeed, would mean a heightening of the coming competition between the two for Mr. Elliot's favour which would give Mrs. Clay greater prominence, as well as taking from the novel what it gains from the manoeuvring with respect to Sir Walter that she and Mr. Elliot are later presumed to be engaged in. And Mrs. Clay herself might have reason to think that her design upon Sir Walter is still not hopeless. But that she has greater cause to revise her policy at Camden Place may be deduced from a feature of her subsequent conduct which Anne becomes conscious of, but whose significance, once more, escapes her. She identifies as suspect in Mr. Elliot his contriving to please all in that house, despite the tempers of its inhabitants being so various. He had, she notes, "appeared completely to see what Mrs. Clay was about, and to hold her in contempt; and yet Mrs. Clay found him as agreeable as any body" (161). This is sound enough where the gentleman's motives are concerned; but it leaves aside any inclination in the lady which the circumstance may denote. She does, indeed, not seem to dislike the man.

The next instance of the kind comes about with a suddenness that leaves Anne in the thick of the fray with scarcely a moment to reflect on what is happening. It is occasioned by nothing more than a slight drizzle of rain in Milsom Street; but the consequence could not be more marked. Shelter in Lady Dalrymple's carriage being the undoubted privilege of Miss Elliot, the remaining seat is at the disposal of one of the other two ladies of the party. Correctly, and politely as ever, Mrs. Clay offers Anne the place: "her civility", as Jane Austen writes with meaning, "rendered her as anxious to be left to walk with Mr. Elliot, as Anne could be". The point is disputed between them with "a generosity so polite, and so determined", in fact – the rain to each being only a trifle, and Mrs. Clay affirming her boots to be "much thicker than Miss Anne's" – that it can only be settled by outside agency, Miss Elliot maintaining that Mrs. Clay has a little cold already, and Mr. Elliot "deciding on appeal, that his cousin Anne's boots were rather the thickest" (174-5). What is evident to the reader from this skirmish, and can only be so to Anne, is the strong desire in Mrs. Clay to be with Mr. Elliot; yet from this open rivalry Anne appears to make no inference as to the state of the other's emotions. – Is it because she is assured of Elliot's preference, reflected in his decision? Or because she regards Mrs. Clay as too far beneath them to be worth considering? Or is the entire incident driven from her mind the next instant, by the sight of Captain Wentworth walking down the street?

Two things at least are clear. Jane Austen will not use what has happened in Milsom Street to do anything that would put Mrs. Clay on a level with Anne, romantically speaking. And Mrs. Clay has learned from Mr. Elliot's action that at this moment he has more interest in Anne than herself.

Needless to say, Mrs. Clay is together with Sir Walter and his two daughters when, the earliest of their party for the concert, they take their position by one of the fires in the Octagon Room. Presently

Captain Wentworth enters alone. Anne boldly steps towards him; and there follows between them a conversation which, despite the door's slam and the "ceaseless buzz of persons walking through" (183), could not fail to impress the others by its length and particularity. It is enough indeed to gain for Wentworth the "simple acknowledgement of acquaintance" formally bestowed on him by Sir Walter and Elizabeth; but it develops into that near-declaration from him which renders Anne "struck, gratified, confused, and beginning to breathe very quick, and feel a hundred things in a moment". Throughout the whole, Anne is too engrossed to have a thought for Mrs. Clay: but the reverse is not true. Mrs. Clay will have seen enough to give her a far stronger hint than that which was soon to suffice for Mrs. Smith, that it is not Mr. Elliot who holds the key to Anne's heart.

The impression will have been confirmed almost immediately afterwards, though, sitting close to them on the "contiguous benches" of the concert room, she is to see Mr. Elliot talking to Anne with almost equal particularity: confusing her with his flattery, professing in low tones an acquaintance with her character long before their meeting, and gaining her curiosity and eager questioning, until a rearrangement of the party separates them. For, upon a hesitant Captain Wentworth then once more approaching, he is determinedly engaged in conversation by Anne for a second time, only to walk off with abruptness at the moment she is touched on the shoulder by Mr. Elliot making a request. Mrs. Clay now is sufficiently in the secret of Anne's affections to know, with gratification, that Mr. Elliot's chance with her is slight: and conscious that Anne is perfectly unaware, amidst the excitements and intimations the evening has brought her, of having betrayed her innermost feelings.

It is but a matter of hours before Anne, discoursing with her friend in Westgate Buildings, is in receipt of information as decisive about the heart of Mr. Elliot, and his business in Bath. The mystery of his eagerness to be reconciled to Sir Walter, and of his constant attendance in Camden Place, is resolved: all has been brought about through the "very material change in Mr. Elliot's opinion as to the value of a baronetcy", and what has become for him the vital need to head off from its present possessor the advances of the "clever, insinuating, handsome woman, poor and plausible" (206), who, according to Mrs. Smith, is laying siege to its honours. But this estimate of Mrs. Clay is from externalities only, based on information gleaned from hearsay and report; and so is the opinion that the threat is lessening because of the lady's awareness that Elliot "sees through her, and not daring to do as she might do in his absence". The bulk of what Mrs. Smith affirms having been proved accurate, it is not surprising that Anne, in her wider ignorance, should take that part appertaining to Mrs. Clay as comprising the extent of her ambition. The design upon Sir Walter is all that she has managed, and, perhaps, cares, to grasp. Thus she will proceed to dismiss simply as good acting the pleasure now so evident in Mrs. Clay at knowledge that Mr. Elliot will be in the house the same evening. She even can admit herself perplexed by the thought that, while "Mrs. Clay must hate the thought of Mr. Elliot", she could yet "assume a most placid, obliging look, and appear quite satisfied with the curtailed license of devoting herself only half as much to Sir Walter as she would have done otherwise" (213-4). The possibility of another, and a deeper, explanation never crosses her mind.

Is it credible that an Anne Elliot, with her intelligence, reflectiveness, and principle, can have been so deceived as to the conduct of one within her circle, and blind in matters of dearest concern? For answer, we have only to look at ourselves. Making wrong inferences from appearances is a common enough pursuit; and Jane Austen's heroines are industriously engaged upon it. We have for example but to think of Emma's surmisings about Jane Fairfax's pianoforte, or Frank Churchill's rescuing Harriet from the gipsies; of Elizabeth Bennet, who before has prided herself upon her discernment, "wretchedly blind" to Darcy's character; or poor Catherine's deduction from General Tilney's having discarded the portrait of his late wife. Were a calculation to be made, it might well appear that, in terms of their more important suppositions, the heroines are nearly as often mistaken as not. Perhaps for them all, the explanation is that which may credibly be given for Anne Elliot:

that she has been too much governed by preconception, and too full of her own affairs and feelings, to be able to discern the reality.

*   *   *

But at least she has learned the truth about Mr. Elliot. It is distressing for her now even to see him, painful to have him speak to her, and be finding insincerity in his every word and gesture. Only one course of action is open to her once she is convinced she has found him out. It is, while avoiding any marked alteration of manners, "to be as decidedly cool to him as might be compatible with their relationship, and to retrace, as quietly as she could, the few steps of unnecessary intimacy she had been gradually led along" (214). For, as she knew from the moment of her leaving Westgate Buildings, there was no longer "any thing of tenderness" due to him – nothing, in fact, of the least concern, politeness apart. But however delicately Anne may have conveyed this disfavour, a "sensible, discerning mind" like Elliot's will be conscious of having experienced a rebuff. He might scarcely have noticed Captain Wentworth at Lyme, or in Milsom Street, and have paid little heed to him at the concert; perhaps he would not yet suspect some new disposition on Anne's part. But the change in her attitude to himself, and his sense of the clouding of his prospect of success with her, will be unmistakable: and will give him reason, and put him at liberty, to pursue a long-developing preference of his own.

This apparently is the cause of his absenting himself for a day or two from Sir Walter's house and its constraints, for a visit to Thornbury, as he lets it be known. Part of the outcome is visible to the entire company at the White Hart, in the phenomenon of his being observed under the colonnade by the corner with Bath Street, "deep in talk" with Mrs. Clay, and then shaking hands with her (the sign of cordiality itself) as they turn from each other in different directions. On moving to the window at Mary Musgrove's insistence, Anne, predictably, is put to "checking the surprise which she could not but feel at such appearance of friendly conference between two persons of totally opposite interests"

(223). She is moved by no very generous impulse that evening to let Mrs. Clay know of her having been seen in Elliot's company three hours after his supposedly leaving Bath. All the satisfaction she gains is the impression of a flash of guilt instantly cleared away, an over-long protestation from the lady of having forgotten their meeting, and a supposition thereupon that, "by some complication of mutual trick, or some overbearing authority of his", she had been obliged to listen to his "lectures and restriction on her designs on Sir Walter" (228). It is this entirely mistaken notion of hers that we are left with. Enlightenment at what has been going on between Mr. Elliot and Mrs. Clay, and about the real state of the lady's affections, Anne Elliot is unable, and Jane Austen has been unwilling, to provide for us.

Anything further concerning the pair is conveyed through narration. We are told that Anne's engagement to Wentworth frustrated any design Mr. Elliot had on Elizabeth, and his plan to resume the watch upon Sir Walter which "a son-in-law's rights would have given him"; but that his "double game" in establishing Mrs. Clay in London reveals a determination "to save himself from being cut out by one woman at least" (250). Succinct as it is, the account is just: but can the same be said of Jane Austen's final words upon Mrs. Clay? That "she had sacrificed, for the younger man's sake, the possibility of scheming longer for Sir Walter", as far as it goes, is correct. But the prefatory statement that "Mrs. Clay's affections had overpowered her interest" begs the question of how much of an interest the baronet still remained for her, after the revelation of his aristocratic fastidiousness, and of the next Sir Walter's amorous inclination towards herself. The concluding comment, perhaps fittingly, leaves her prospects with Mr. Elliot as a subject for conjecture; but the laconic admission that Mrs. Clay "has abilities, however, as well as affections" may be regarded as testimony to whatever, in her enforced reluctance, the author has left unexplored or undivulged regarding this character.

For her attitude throughout – only half-acknowledged, doubtless, even to herself – is that the penniless daughter of a lawyer, however otherwise gifted in mind and manners, is not to be viewed as acceptable by society's norms, as they are embodied in the novels, and were present by and large in the minds of contemporary readers. Jane Austen has been anything but lavish in depicting Mrs. Clay; has presented her to us mainly through the critical eyes of her rival, and minimally, even so. But the meeting by the Pump Room shows that the lady had inspired in Mr. Elliot an attachment more certain and real than that he entertained for Anne Elliot – which he had never reached the stage of professing, despite his manifold attentions to her. And from the little we do know of Mrs. Clay – from an appreciation we come at length to share with her literary creator – we are assured she is by no means so common as her name might suggest: and will display more elegance and true personableness in her future role as Lady Elliot, than a Lady Dalrymple, or a Lady Catherine de Bourgh, or a Lady Bertram, is able to bring to her respective position in society. Not to mention Mrs. Ferrars.

Perhaps this is what the disadvantaged rebel within Jane Austen was wanting to say as part of the unwritten story in *Persuasion*. How much of it would have been revealed, one wonders, if the first reference to the novel in her Letters, on March 13th, 1817 – "I have something ready for Publication, which may perhaps appear about a twelvemonth hence"[32] – was a hint of intended revision?

# iii

# Elizabeth and Mr. Bennet

"They have none of them much to recommend them", declares Mr. Bennet of his five daughters; "they are all silly and ignorant like other girls; but Lizzy has something more of quickness than her sisters". With this reflection upon his own flesh and blood he assails the susceptibilities of his wife, with predictable success. What in particular will incense Mrs. Bennet is the preference openly affirmed in this remark, and in the "good word for my little Lizzy" that he has made so bold as to "throw in".

Elizabeth, as she and her father are well aware, is the "least dear" to her mother of all her children, as the author states it. Who is to say that Mrs. Bennet's resort, in her befuddled consciousness of being the butt of her husband's ridicule, is not to take it out of the sibling who is most like him in critical propensity? But equally involuntary, we may also infer, is Mr. Bennet's confession of regard, indeed, affection, for his second daughter: yet one more instance of a truth being spoken in jest, even by a person customarily as undemonstrative as he.

That roundness in the creation of characters which is the hallmark of dramatic and literary achievement extends, in Jane Austen's writing, to the whole families from which they spring, attributes of the elders being present or reflected in varying proportion in the children: a fact often noted and intriguingly explored. Certainly, Elizabeth displays a decided likeness to her mother in her tendency to indignant expostulation, and, if not ignorance of them, momentary forgetfulness of the demands of the polite conventions. But this is little more than a trick of temperament, in comparison with the substantial qualities of personality which show her so evidently to be her father's daughter.

One respect in which she seems not at all to resemble Mr. Bennet is in his aloofness and imperturbability both as to persons and events. What we soon learn about the lesser detail of his everyday dealings is indication enough. He takes little if any interest in his neighbours, is with a book regardless of time, and pays social functions the compliment of absenting himself from them. The invitation from the newcomers, the Bingleys, to the ball at Netherfield Park must perforce be accepted; but the diversion it affords him is not of the kind that such gatherings would normally be thought to promote. It consists in watching with silent enjoyment, and entire absence of embarrassment, the gaucheries and discomfiture of his own family, from Mr. Collins's bizarre address to the company on the duties of a cleric, and Mary's distressing endeavours at the pianoforte, to Lydia's all too natural yawnings, and the repulse by their disdainful and wearied hosts of his wife's obtuse civilities.

His manner at Longbourn House during the uproar which follows Elizabeth's rejection of Mr. Collins differs not a whit from that he has displayed at Netherfield. When the distrait Mrs. Bennet bursts into his library, he fixes his eyes on her "with a calm unconcern which was not in the least altered by her communication", and expresses itself in the remote and ironic courtesy of, "I have not the pleasure of understanding you. Of what are you talking?" (111) And his first instinct, when the state of affairs is spelled out to him, is to detach himself from it, despite its consequence for the family: "And what am I to do on the occasion? – It seems an hopeless business". His words here belie his intention, which, as it turns out, is most purposeful; but the coolness with which they are delivered aptly denotes a man whose relationship to his own wife is one of being "very little otherwise indebted, than as her ignorance and folly had contributed to his amusement" (236).

No such distance from people and happenings close at hand is observable in his daughter. It is on the contrary only natural in a young woman of Elizabeth's vivacity that she should be intimately involved in her immediate world. Yet she does display a capacity for detachment amidst its impressions and demands which must be seen as estimable, and notably contributes to making her the person she is. Nowhere is it more evident than after she has looked in vain for Wickham at the Netherfield ball, and learned that his absence is due indirectly to Darcy's influence. For a moment her disappointment, and its accompanying anger, is extreme. But, we are told, she was not formed for ill-humour: this destruction of her own pleasure for the evening "could not dwell long on her spirits", and was soon deliberately made to yield place to the recreation of pointing out Mr. Collins's oddities to Charlotte Lucas. Another vexation closer to home is similarly assuaged. Though her appeal to Mr. Bennet concerning Lydia's unbridled behaviour scarcely gains a hearing, she departs from the interview with equanimity. A consciousness of having done her duty helps to sustain her; but more flows from the fact that "to fret over unavoidable evils, or augment them by anxiety, was no part of her disposition" (232). Her aunt Mrs. Gardiner is right in judging that it would have been better if Jane's being jilted had happened to Elizabeth, since she would have laughed herself out of it sooner.

The same attribute enables her to be relaxed in the unfamiliar surroundings at Rosings. As the little party draws near to it, she is troubled by none of those apprehensions which afflict two of her companions, from a certainty alike that Lady Catherine has nothing extraordinary about her, and that "the mere stateliness of money and rank" was something she herself "could witness without trepidation". She is, in consequence, equal to the scene within. That at Hunsford Parsonage when Darcy is making his declaration is more threatening. There, Elizabeth is beset with emotions, strong and conflicting – with shock and embarrassment, with dislike, gratitude and resentment – but she is by no means overwhelmed by them while he remains, or in any degree deprived of her usual ability to see and think clearly. The inflexibility of her opinion of Darcy, true enough, might well have enabled her to retain a proper perspective; but it is not insignificant nevertheless that, despite the surprise, the lover's urgency, the greatness of the offer and the tumult of her own feelings, "she could easily see that he had no doubt of a favourable answer", despite his professions of anxiety (189).

\* \* \*

A capacity to distance oneself from the immediacy of event and the threat of emotion's dominance, necessarily an individual trait, is most often the distinguishing feature of a very able mind. Ability, Mr. Bennet and Elizabeth possess in plenty; and in both of them it manifests itself in a certain formality or methodicalness of approach in matters of judgment and within their own mental processes: what might be termed a precision, or a principled way of thinking. Thus, for all his laxity and indolence of disposition, and his straightened means, we would never be tempted to doubt Mr. Bennet's declaration that, had the financial settlement with Wickham been Elizabeth's uncle's doing, "I must and *would* have paid him". This same punctiliousness might be thought to inform his estimate of Mr. Collins as a suitor, and his manner of conveying it to Elizabeth after Mrs. Bennet's ultimatum. "From this day you must be a stranger to one of your parents. – Your mother will never see you again if you do *not* marry Mr. Collins, and I will never see you again if you *do*". And it is surely to be detected in the more serious circumstance of his trying to dissuade her from yoking herself to the "proud, unpleasant" Mr. Darcy. After the initial astonishment he is as deeply moved in the endeavour as father can be; but he has first, with what may be regarded as a laudable paternal rectitude, given his daughter his consent upon her tearful assurance of her affection for the man she has chosen (376-7).

The principled approach is more evident in Elizabeth, if only for the reason that we see more of her than her father. Even in so very personal a discussion as that between Jane and herself on the conduct of Charlotte Lucas in accepting Mr. Collins, Elizabeth's eloquence is engaged not so much in presenting the attitude she has formed as upon defining the concepts it embodies.

> "You shall not defend her, though it is Charlotte Lucas. You shall not, for the sake of one individual, change the meaning of principle and integrity, nor endeavour to persuade yourself

or me, that selfishness is prudence, and insensibility to danger, security for happiness" (135-6).

And though such severity of emphasis might be imagined to have no place in episodes of laughter and happiness, there is a rare delightfulness in the question to Darcy after their betrothal as to the seemliness of her disclosing to him her knowledge of what he had done for Lydia, in the hope that it would bring on his proposal.

> "My resolution of thanking you for your kindness to Lydia had certainly great effect. *Too much*, I am afraid; for what becomes of the moral, if our comfort springs from a breach of promise, for I ought not to have mentioned the subject?" (381)

This propensity to detach the significance from the happening, and to view it in its abstraction as perhaps the greater reality, is present in the lightest instances of Elizabeth's conversation and reflection. Jane's deploring the disappointment Darcy must have suffered upon being so unceremoniously rejected provokes from her the mock-assertion that its effect is to render her correspondingly indifferent and unconcerned. "Your profusion makes me saving; and if you lament over him much longer, my heart will be as light as a feather". After this conversation she is left thinking about the disclosure in Darcy's letter of Bingley's affection for her sister, which she cannot mention to her until there is perfect understanding between the parties: in which presumptive event Bingley is far better suited to be the informant. Between frustration and mirth, she tells herself, "The liberty of communication cannot be mine until it has lost all its value!" – ending, characteristically, with a syllogism (225-7).

For it is in much the same way upon the logic, or lack of it, in the position taken by Mrs. Gardiner with respect to Wickham's new-found interest in Miss King since her acquisition of £10,000, that Elizabeth has pronounced with such peremptory frankness. Her aunt had suggested a venal motive in Wickham, and frowned upon Miss King's acceptance of his hasty attentions. Elizabeth, struck by Mrs. Gardiner's past warning her against an imprudent match with him, and present condemnation of his seeking a fortune upon which to marry, is moved to defend both persons. An impoverished young man, she argues, has not time for the "elegant decorums"; and if the lady herself is content, none can reasonably make objection. But the continuance of her aunt's disapproval provokes her to impatience with inconsistency, even in someone she is so fond of. "Well," she cries, "have it as you choose. *He* shall be mercenary, and *she* shall be foolish" (153).

\* \* \*

Elizabeth Bennet is shown to be as susceptible to her feelings as are any of us. But she is unusual in that their very potency can quicken her thinking into new orderliness. The last place where one would expect to find this aptitude is in her angry dialogue with Darcy, but it is most evident there. The final affront – indeed, insult – of his passionate reference to her family's social inferiority induces only the contrasting reserve of her stating that the mode of his declaration merely spares her the concern she would have felt had his behaviour been more gentlemanlike. What follows is like nothing so much as the stages of a reasoned case. In no way could she have been tempted to accept him; the arrogance of his disposition noted on early acquaintance had formed a "ground-work of disapprobation"; and upon this basis succeeding knowledge of him had built an "immovable" dislike. It is only when the successive charges reach their unequivocal conclusion that emotion finds scope in the rather less controlled affirmation of his being "the last man in the world whom I could ever be prevailed on to marry" (193).

An innate tendency to consider the behaviour of others and oneself in terms of the principles underlying it will present rather starkly to its possessor the strange contrarieties and anomalies that subsist in social norms and in the human lot generally. To this kind of awareness Elizabeth is at all times prone; and it accounts for a charmingly philosophical element in her make-up which guards against any waywardness on her part, while endearing her to the reader. When, for example, the object they have all longed for is secured in the arrangements for Wickham's marriage to Lydia, Elizabeth rejoices; but in an instant her mood has changed to a near-horror at the implications: "And they *must* marry! Yet he is *such* a man" (304). She is astonished by the strangeness of their present joy, and need for thankfulness, at the prospect of a union which will afford no chance of happiness, and in which the profligate inclination of the husband is a certainty. But the vagaries of her own dealings can come under as critical a scrutiny; for, with such thinking, there is no room for evasion or dissimulation in one's contemplation of them. It will exact the penalty of always "Doubting sad end of principle unsound", wherever such principle may reside. How ruefully Elizabeth considers her past rashness with respect to Darcy after he has taken his leave at Lambton, as she throws "a retrospective glance over their whole acquaintance, so full of contradictions and varieties, and sighed at the perverseness of those feelings which would now have promoted its continuance, and would formerly have rejoiced at its termination" (279).

\*   \*   \*

What, we might wonder, is the quality of Mr. Bennet's brooding thoughts? He may be as well equipped for introspection as his daughter, though, one suspects, less given to the practice from the consequences of an unsuitable marriage. Happily for them both, however, it is the external sphere which commands their main interest, and provides their greatest pleasure; and it is for the outward aspect of things, further, that their keenly analytical powers of mind make them both suited. In Mr. Bennet they are elsewhere directed while, tiring of his family, he devotes himself to his books; but his ability quickly to grasp and see through a situation when occasion demands it is impressive. Talking with Elizabeth about Jane's disappointment, and offering only the dubious consolation that, next to being married, "a girl likes to be crossed in love a little now and then", he asks her when her turn is to come, and with prophetic insight urges, "Let Wickham be *your* man. He is a pleasant fellow, and would jilt you creditably" (137). The same perceptiveness determines that the provisions set out in Mr. Gardiner's letter for Wickham and Lydia's marriage conceal the chief fact of money having been put down. "Wickham's a fool, if he takes her with a farthing less than ten thousand pounds", he affirms; with contemptuous solicitude then adding, "I should be sorry to think so ill of him, in the very beginning of our relationship" (304).

Such mental achievement Elizabeth can readily equal. Had she not straight away seen from the pompous style and needless apology in the letter from Mr. Collins read out to the family that their clerical cousin must be an oddity? And does she not, contradicting her uncle's hopes of an intention in the eloping couple to marry in London, deduce the worst from the secrecy, and fear of detection in their disappearance, and from the one's need of money and the other's inability to supply it, and unreservedly affirm, "Oh! No, no, this is not likely"? As swift, and correct, is her judgment that in the Bingley sisters' estimation the Bennets are "not rich enough, or grand enough for them"; or, when once shut in her room at the Parsonage, that Col. Fitzwilliam must have been referring to Bingley as the friend Darcy had recently saved from making an imprudent marriage, since "There could not exist in the world *two* men, over whom Mr. Darcy could have such boundless influence" (186).

There is nothing remarkable in Elizabeth's crediting, despite strong initial reservations, the whole of the studied and detailed account of his actions that Darcy had set out in the communication he puts into her hand in the park at Rosings. That the affair of his relation with Wickham "was capable of a turn which must make him entirely blameless throughout the whole" would have been evident in any careful perusal. But what is worthy of note is the rapidity with which she ranges through their entire acquaintance and applies this possibility to her own previous suppositions. The impropriety of Wickham's confidences at a first encounter; the unreliability of subsequent professions; the insincerities detectable in his attentions to Miss King, and to herself; the confidence of a man like Bingley in Darcy's being blameless; the lack of any sign of the unprincipled or the unjust in Darcy, for all his repellent manners: all these contrary tokens are immediately before her. Though unable to overcome her fixed disapproval of the man who has made it, the revelation heightens her chagrin at the indecorum of her family, and acquaints her with a novel and demoralizing dissatisfaction with her own conduct.

Her humiliation is the more profound because she had herself anticipated and all but reached the assessment of Wickham that Darcy puts before her. But for the charm of first liking and the flattery of his attentions, the flaws she had detected in Wickham's intimations would have been further dwelt on, and probably led to disbelief; puzzlement, at least, they do bring about in her. Again and again during their discussion at the Phillipses, she exclaims in surprise and wonder at what she is being required to accept as truth. "Good heavens! but how could *that* be?" is her justified reaction to the idea of so definite an intention as the gift of a living being set aside at Darcy's instigation. The plea of his jealousy and dislike of the companion of his youth, Elizabeth can doubt from her own limited experience. "I had supposed him to be despising his fellow-creatures in general, but did not suspect him of descending to such malicious revenge, such injustice, such inhumanity as this!" The known fact of Darcy's pride is here not persuasive. She has found it insufferable, and levelled scorn at it while a guest at Netherfield; but she speaks her incomprehension that pride itself had not constrained him to be just – "If from no better motive, that he should not have been too proud to be dishonest, – for dishonesty I must call it". And, pondering the question while other subjects are being reviewed, she suddenly ventures upon it once more, in surprise that an assured relationship should subsist between Darcy and Bingley. "How can Mr. Bingley, who seems good humour itself", she asks, "and is, I really believe, truly amiable, be in friendship with such a man? How can they suit each other?" Her queries gain answers from Wickham that are sufficiently plausible; but the whole conversation testifies to

Elizabeth's perspicacity. She has come close to detecting Wickham for what he is in the very process of his gaining her affections (79-82).

Analysis of her own feelings, not surprisingly, she finds much more difficult; and, indeed, is entirely capable of being at a loss when it is essential she should be clear. The change in Darcy's manner, when they meet by accident at Pemberley for the first time since their stormy interview in Hunsford Parsonage, is something the reader might think she should at once understand; but, amazed as she is at the striking alteration in him, she has no idea what to attribute it to: "She knew not what to think, nor how to account for it" (252). The principled nature of her thinking is perhaps the reason for her failure, the assured grounds of her past aversion to the man and estimate of the effect upon him of her denunciation combining to preclude the possibility of affection as a cause. And, after the visit in Derbyshire from the Pemberley party, Elizabeth is so unsure of her feelings respecting him that "she lay awake two whole hours, endeavouring to make them out": methodically dismissing hatred and dislike, admitting respect, allowing esteem, and venturing at last to contemplate the presence of gratitude. But nothing at all hinders her capacity later on to see through the complexities of their earlier acquaintance, and determine exactly what it was that had made Darcy admire and fall in love with her.

> "The fact is, that you were sick of civility, of deference, of officious attention. You were disgusted with the women who were always speaking and looking, and thinking for *your* approbation alone. I roused, and interested you, because I was so unlike *them*." (380)

Is she not perfectly right?

*   *   *

When, in the throes of her nervous discontent at the thought of being denied formal introduction to the new owner of Netherfield Park, Mrs. Bennet falls to berating her next-youngest daughter, Mr.

Bennet comments to the assembled family on Kitty's lack of discretion in her coughs: "she times them ill", he declares. But upon his wife's recovering composure and good humour through his announcement of having paid the necessary visit, he gravely advises, as if the paroxysm were voluntary, "Now, Kitty, you may cough as much as you chuse". The novel shows him a master of laconic and sardonic utterance; but it conveys also the reason for his being so, in his vigour of mind and instant apprehension, the "quick parts" whimsically demonstrated in the opening discourse with Mrs. Bennet. This degree of mental capacity itself accounts for that strongly developed sense of the inconsistent and incongruous in human relationships which makes for and gives force to the well-judged terse remark, expressive as it is of an underlying mirth. Thus his wife's detestation of the man who is next in the entail of the estate, and dispossessor of the mother and daughters she is incapable of seeing as any other than its rightful beneficiaries, brings from him the unstinted concurrence of, "It certainly is a most iniquitous affair, and nothing can clear Mr. Collins from the guilt of inheriting Longbourn" (62). In the act of diplomatically putting an end to Mary's endeavours at the pianoforte he cannot forbear the briefest hint as to their significance, in his, "That will do extremely well, child. You have delighted us long enough. Let the other young ladies have time to exhibit". And his method of bringing solace to Mrs. Bennet, in her wilful desolation at the notion of living to see Charlotte Lucas become mistress of Longbourn, is to put before her a neglected contingency which would spare her such distress. "My dear, do not give way to such gloomy thoughts. Let us hope for better things. Let us flatter ourselves that *I* may be the survivor" (130).

It is the same suppressed laughter which prompts an equally ceremonious rejoinder from Elizabeth when Lady Catherine de Bourgh, sweeping aside its mistress's prerogatives, insists that she stay longer at Hunsford Parsonage. "I am much obliged to your ladyship for your kind invitation, but it is not in my power to accept it". As toneless and proper a response is forthcoming from her when Mrs. Bennet, in her indignation at the report of Darcy's having deemed her daughter

"Not handsome enough to dance with!" seriously advises, "Another time, Lizzy, I would not dance with *him*, if I were you". Darcy's asking her, and her taking the unheard-of liberty of asking him, being both seemingly precluded, Elizabeth is nothing but correct in solemnly replying, "I believe, Ma'am, I may safely promise you *never* to dance with him" (20).

Darcy and his associates fare no differently when she is in their company. The affront which the former has perhaps unknowingly administered, and Elizabeth's sense of the pretentiousness prevailing amongst them, Bingley alone excepted, contrive if anything to lend her remarks a greater brevity and emphasis. Darcy's unexpectedly offering her his hand as a partner upon Sir William Lucas's over-enthusiastic recommendation, with its accompanying assurance of the gentleman's having no objection to dancing with her, for all his dislike of the amusement in general, draws from her the astringent compliment of, "Mr. Darcy is all politeness". As ironic is her amused entry to the conversation at Netherfield about handwriting that arises from Miss Bingley's admiration for Darcy's epistolary skills, and denigration of her brother's. Bingley does not deny the charge that he writes "in the most careless way imaginable", and cheerfully confesses to a flow of thoughts so rapid that his letters sometimes convey no ideas at all to his correspondents. Elizabeth's contribution of the simple, "Your humility, Mr. Bingley, must disarm reproof", dispraising both handwriting and implicit boast, brings Darcy into the fray, and leads to that confrontation between the two keenest minds present whose ending is no less than a relief to the rest of them. But it is one of short duration. The rudeness of the sisters next day, in having Darcy as their escort on a narrow path and leaving Elizabeth to walk by herself, brings from her a succinct pronouncement that is amply critical, but withering in its incorporation of Gilpin's classic commonplace as to the number of cows for an aesthetically pleasing tableau: "No, no; stay where you are. –You are charmingly group'd, and appear to uncommon advantage. The picturesque would be spoilt by admitting a fourth" (48-53).

Darcy had noted, and tried to do away, his friends' incivility; but he is destined, for all his dawning tenderness towards their guest, to be treated to some of the most intelligible of her brief utterances. He himself, by unwisely claiming to have sought to avoid such weaknesses in character as can invite ridicule, creates that demur in Elizabeth which gives rise to her sardonic, "Such as vanity and pride"; and Miss Bingley's disdainful inquiry as to the result of her examination of her idol serves only to inspire the derisive acquiescence of, "I am perfectly convinced by it that Mr. Darcy has no defect. He owns it himself without disguise" (57). And not yet is she finished with him. Any of his failings, as she will designate them to be, is a mark for her to tilt at; and their next encounter, at Rosings, supplies one, in his offering in defence of his having danced only with members of his own party at the ball in Meryton, the plea of not having been acquainted with any other lady in the assembly. "True", Elizabeth replies; "and nobody can ever be introduced in a ball room" (175). Darcy proceeds to explain himself at length; but, with such an opponent, he will not expect to get the better of the exchange. Fortunately, admiration of the lady renders it no issue. What she will have to say to him when he proposes will be as explicit, but more fluent and expansive than the remarks just cited, and so come into another category.

But her greatest triumph in the laconic art is reserved for her former admirer, George Wickham. After her return from Hunsford, he inquires as to her visit; and, learning that she had met Darcy and Col. Fitzwilliam there, observes with some temerity that the latter's manners are very different from those of his cousin. "Yes, very different", Elizabeth agrees composedly. "But I think Mr. Darcy improves on acquaintance". In apprehension as to her meaning, Wickham jocularly suggests that the improvement is in civility, rather than in essentials. Again, there is the terse seeming accord of, "Oh no! In essentials, I believe, he is very much what he ever was". In his disquiet at the drift of her words, Wickham can only look for some clue in her expression, while she amplifies these brief statements in terms of such neutrality as can only intensify his alarm.

"When I said that he improved on acquaintance, I did not mean that either his mind or manners were in a state of improvement, but that from knowing him better, his disposition was better understood."

So has Elizabeth by these minimal remarks paid off scores for past deceptions, that the two of them part at last "with mutual civility, and possibly a mutual desire of never meeting again" (234-5).

\* \* \*

"I dearly love a laugh", Elizabeth confides to the company at Netherfield; and, to make matters clearer, adds, "Follies and nonsense, whims and inconsistencies *do* divert me, I own, and I laugh at them whenever I can" (56). Her confession has been prompted by Miss Bingley's certainty of there being nothing in Darcy's disposition capable of giving rise to laughter – a possibility which for Elizabeth is itself a delicious piece of nonsense, as she thereupon gives him to understand. It is this idiosyncrasy which has ensured her not being long dismayed when Darcy declares her no more than "tolerable" at their first meeting. Though harbouring "no very cordial feelings towards him", she is soon with much merriment telling the story among her friends; "for", we then learn, "she had a lively, playful disposition, which delighted in any thing ridiculous" (12). Life clearly provides for her a plenitude of such objects. Caroline Bingley's commendation of Darcy's letter-writing had kept her "sufficiently amused"; the sight of Sir William Lucas stationed in the doorway of the Parsonage in earnest contemplation of the greatness before him in the phaeton at the gate, "and constantly bowing whenever Miss De Bourgh looked that way", sustains Elizabeth in "high diversion"; and she is reduced to such helplessness by the idea of the solemn Mr. Collins being run away with by his feelings as to be incapacitated from halting him in his amorous declaration. Nor is it the more obvious follies, at moments of ease, that charm her. In the very midst of the embarrassment of having to introduce Mr. and

Mrs. Gardiner in the grounds of Pemberley to their owner, she cannot resist "a sly look at him, to see how he bore it" in going through the formidable ritual, and the half expectation "of his decamping as fast as he could from such disgraceful companions" (255).

That this characteristic in Elizabeth is a paternal endowment is beyond doubt; indeed, it is what closely unites the two, as we see for instance from the looks and glances they exchange when first exposed to Mr. Collins's conversation. Mr. Bennet's "resolute composure of countenance" masks "the keenest enjoyment" he finds in the guest who has answered all his hopes of being the very reverse of a sensible man, and thus is, by his own definition, "a valuable acquaintance". Not with dismay, but with the same glee as Elizabeth is to view Sir William's bowings, does he greet Collins's egregious peroration at the Netherfield ball: no-one there "looked more amused than Mr. Bennet himself". Elizabeth, one suspects, cannot evince such reverential delight at follies and nonsense; the very brainlessness of his own spouse is the source of endless pleasure for him. Tenderly he considers her incomprehension of the legalities by which the Collinses are to become the possessors of Longbourn. "If it was not for the entail", she has pronounced to him, "I should not mind it". The gentle question, "What should you not mind?" secures for Mr. Bennet the answer he has ardently hoped for: "I should not mind any thing at all". With profound satisfaction, both intellectual and comical, he serenely concludes, "Let us be thankful that you are preserved from a state of such insensibility" (130).

\*   \*   \*

The fact that his dearest daughter cannot accompany him into the highest flights of humour is explained by Mr. Bennet's having irresponsibly almost withdrawn from family life, as from that of society round about him. His wife's maladroitness in both contexts means for him nothing other than amusement; in the closer concerns she is no real hindrance, being capable of little more bothersome than a querulous compliance. But with Elizabeth it is otherwise. In her situation as the second of five almost dowerless sisters, family affairs are components of her destiny, and the mother presiding over them a force – erratic, and often perverse – to be reckoned with. Mrs. Bennet's excesses cause Elizabeth not only embarrassment but anxiety: as when, blushing for her, she tries in vain to end her attack on Darcy for what she takes to be his contempt for country living; or, at supper during the ball at Netherfield, with "inexpressible vexation" to interrupt the flow of her mother's self-congratulation at the prospect of Jane's engagement from reaching and offending Darcy sitting opposite. "What is Mr. Darcy to me, pray, that I should be afraid of him?" is the very audible response. "I am sure we owe him no such particular civility as to be obliged to say nothing *he* may not like to hear" (99). Not only by Mrs. Bennet's actions is Elizabeth's task made uncomfortable, and occasionally distressing: she has also to endeavour "to forget what she could not overlook" in her father's treatment of her, and so "banish from her thoughts that continual breach of conjugal obligation and decorum" which daily exposed her mother to the contempt of her children. Tested as she is, it is not as easy for her mind as for her father's to register and contemplate the humorous aspects of existence in their purity (236).

She is unable, therefore, to express an unqualified agreement to Mr. Bennet's question, "For what do we live, but to make sport of our neighbours, and laugh at them in our turn?" Nor, what is more, greatly value his comment upon Jane's disappointment over Bingley, "that, whatever of that kind may befal you, you have an affectionate mother who will always make the most of it" (138). Though quite capable in her livelier moments of causing it, she is not free to enjoy social disharmony; nor, with a becoming modesty, is she so given to abandoning scruple as to seek to provoke and expose folly in the way her father does. His method, often enough, is by the type of mocking query Mrs. Bennet correctly terms tiresome or nonsensical: like the, "How so? how can it affect them?" in response to her exclaiming, "What a fine thing for our girls!" at Bingley's coming to Netherfield Park; and the, "Is that his design in settling here?" upon her explanation that she is thinking of his marrying one of them.

Mr. Bennet's questioning is at its most sinister when it has the appearance of being judicially serious; as when Mr. Collins, elaborating upon "those little delicate compliments" he considers ladies to enjoy, and himself to be gifted in presenting, is told that he judges very properly, and politely asked "whether these pleasing attentions proceed from the impulse of the moment, or are the result of previous study?" (68) But the apparently casual and innocent observation can with equal effect serve as prelude to folly's enactment. The assurance that she is as handsome as any of her daughters, producing from Mrs. Bennet an affected disclaimer on the plea of a grown up family, gains for her the knavish speech of, "In such cases, a woman has not often much beauty to think of" that will, mercifully, sleep in her foolish ear. And his mere remarking of the hat Elizabeth is engaged in trimming that he hopes Mr. Bingley will like it, introduces the singular episode of the girls' bewilderment and their mother's expostulation which ends with the latter's, "I am sick of Mr. Bingley", Mr. Bennet's announcement, full of pretended dismay, of acquaintance with him having already been established, and his departure in fatigued contentment at the domestic squall so induced and allayed.

Elizabeth admittedly makes an attempt in this kind, but she is incited thereto by high spirits, and, falling short of the finesse in which her father excels, rather comes to grief. Impelled by the surge of happiness that runs through the family when the invitation to the ball at Netherfield is given, she mischievously inquires of Mr. Collins "whether he intended to accept Mr. Bingley's invitation, and if he did, whether he would think it proper to join in the evening's amusement". The outcome, in combination with a wordy affirmative, is a request for her hand for the first two dances that she has no choice but to accept with as good grace as she can muster (87).

\* \* \*

Behind the enjoyment of follies and nonsense lies a developed appreciation of incongruity; and this, in turn, as it relates to character and conduct, necessarily implies the perception of fault. And since the social milieu possesses more meaning for Elizabeth than for her father, it is as natural that she should exhibit a greater readiness than he to direct blame, and in fact to confront an offender. Thus there is to be found in her a type of ready remonstrance to which Mr. Bennet is hardly drawn. It exists in her meaningfully presenting to Mr. Darcy the twin vices of vanity and pride as failings to be guarded against, and in her more vigorous challenge of, "But these, I suppose, are precisely what you are without" (57). She has previously defended Bingley's self-declared easiness of temper, and attacked Darcy's studied disrespect for it, in her cry to the latter, "You have shewn him off now much more than he did himself". Such criticisms, while pointed enough, are the incidental products of discussion; but in her dealings with George Wickham, Elizabeth does not flinch from the strictest confrontation. When he asks concerning the old housekeeper at Pemberley, she is not restrained from reporting her adverse comment upon him, with the sarcastic observation, "At such a distance as *that*, you know, things are strangely misinterpreted". Her aim, be it said, is to silence him; but, not succeeding, she proceeds to put a stop to his reflections on the clerical life he claims has been denied him, with the facts about the forfeited living she has learned from Darcy. And she counters his facetious reference to the making of sermons with the incisive, "I *did* hear, too, that there was a time, when sermon-making was not so palatable to you as it seems to be at present; that you actually declared your resolution of never taking orders, and that the business had been compromised accordingly". Then, as if her moral ascendancy had not been complete, she imposes it with a change of direction as masterly in its way as anything Mr. Bennet has ever accomplished.

> "Come, Mr. Wickham, we are brother and sister, you know. Do not let us quarrel about the past. In future, I hope we shall be always of one mind."

At this, she holds out her hand. Wickham kisses it, the author tells us, "with affectionate gallantry"; but the fact that when so engaged "he hardly knew how to look" can occasion no surprise (327-9).

She has administered – executed is perhaps the better word – a "set down". Of this gentle art, Mr. Bennet is, by his wife's report, and the single example he provides for us, a consummate practitioner. The recommendation he sends Mr. Collins that, while consoling Lady Catherine at the news of Elizabeth's engagement to Darcy, he should stand by the nephew, since "He has more to give", is as potent as his daughter's, but superior in being so much more economical. The disadvantage he is under, of having to conquer a reluctance to exert himself in this or any other way, is not present in Elizabeth. She has been so liberal in these attentions as to set upon a startled Lady Catherine within her own fastness at Rosings on the subject of a daughter's "coming out", with the unheard-of proposition that "The last born has as good a right to the pleasures of youth, as the first"; for better measure appending, on the assumption of the elder's being unwilling or unable to marry, the insufferable, "And to be kept back on *such* a motive!" (165) For his pains in frankly confessing the normal inability of a younger son "to marry without some attention to money", Col. Fitzwilliam is rewarded with the derisive, "And pray, what is the usual price of an Earl's younger son? Unless the elder brother is very sickly, I suppose you would not ask above fifty thousand pounds" (184).

The personal note present here has, naturally enough, already been repeatedly sounded in Elizabeth's acrimonious dealings with Darcy. At Netherfield, her making at first no response to his invitation to dance a reel with him is explained as the confounding of a wish on his part to despise her taste; "but", she tells him, "I always delight in overthrowing those kind of schemes, and cheating a person of their premeditated contempt" (52). His advancing in stately manner at Rosings while she is at the pianoforte earns him a similar rebuff. This time his intention can only be to frighten her, but she will not be alarmed: "My courage always rises with every attempt to intimidate me". These set downs are in fact accusations, though they lack the denunciatory vehemence of her offering while a guest at Netherfield, when, on Darcy's going so far as to concede that every disposition must have some natural and ineradicable defect, she exclaims, "And *your* defect is a propensity to hate every body" (58). But even this is a trifle compared to her charges at Hunsford Parsonage; the substance of what she has to say there, if it is anything, is one extensive and strident set down. She makes atonement for it in due course by accepting Darcy as her husband; but that she has no intention of abandoning this notable expertise is apparent when, calling upon him, with proper feminine curiosity, to account for having fallen in love with her, she reminds him of their initial encounter with, "My beauty you had early withstood" (380). It is a set down of superb quality, the more so for its being spoken in jest.

\* \* \*

As with so many manifestations in father and daughter, it is the fundamental excellence of their minds that promotes and pervades them. And their quick recognition of failings in others is more than matched by the rigour with which realisation of their own shortcomings affects them. Both are victims of transient moods of bitter self-accusation and depression. Mr. Bennet is transfixed by guilt upon Lydia's infamous elopement. "I never saw any one so shocked", Jane reports of his reaction. "He could not speak a word for full ten minutes". And he so far interrupts the composure he has reassumed by the time of his return from London as to decline Elizabeth's proffer of sympathy for what he has gone through. "Say nothing of that", he declares. "Who should suffer but myself? It has been my own doing, and I ought to feel it"; adding, however, for their mutual comfort, the assurance, born of self-knowledge, that far from the impression's being able to overpower him, "It will pass away soon enough" (299).

Less severe, possibly, at the time, but longer-lasting, has been Elizabeth's self-reproach when awareness comes of how "blind, partial, prejudiced, absurd" she has been in her relation with Darcy and Wickham. What makes worse her suffering at the discovery is recognition that it is in direct proportion to the high esteem in which before she had held herself. "I, who have prided myself on my discernment!" she cries. " – I, who have valued myself on my abilities!" From such comprehension there can be no escape – and relief only in the truth of its being "how just a humiliation!" (208) So also she views her share of responsibility for what has happened with Lydia, upon the news of the elopement. Certainty that she might have prevented it overcomes all that she feels at this moment for herself, and for Darcy who attends her. The compelling thought is of her failure to take action despite the recently-acquired knowledge of Wickham's character: of the "Wretched, wretched mistake!" Like her father, in a different circumstance, she must admit the full force of blame.

\* \* \*

What distinguishes the love between Mr. Bennet and his daughter, and makes it as admirable as it is affecting, is its clear-sightedness. There is no vestige of sentimentality in it. Their relationship is founded upon full knowledge – which, on one side at least, is often wished less. However different by kinship and convention their status might be, and unlike their usual employments and concerns, in intellect they are equals: and it is as equals that they respond to each other. When her father, accurately surmising a personal motive, dismisses out of hand her warning to him of "the very great disadvantage to us all", as she puts it, of Lydia's flirtatious behaviour, Elizabeth, too, puts courtesy aside, and gives him without embellishment her opinion of his neglect of paternal duty. "Excuse me – for I must speak plainly. If you, my dear father, will not take the trouble of checking her exuberant spirits, and of teaching her that her present pursuits are not to be the business of her life, she will soon be beyond the reach of amendment" (230-1). Thus is rebuke given, and received, where reciprocal understanding is complete. Roles are reversed when Mr. Bennet, under the impression Elizabeth has consented to marry a man she dislikes for the sake of his wealth, greets her with the greater plainness of, "Are you out of your senses, to be accepting this man?" and answers her faltering assurance of sincere attachment to Mr. Darcy with the scorn of, "Or in other words, you are determined to have him. He is rich, to be sure". The tone and substance of what he has to say to her change dramatically once the reality of the bond between them is apparent to him; but his advice that it be broken, though to a daughter, has the candour of the truest comradeship.

> "I know your disposition, Lizzy. I know that you could be neither happy nor respectable, unless you truly esteemed your husband; unless you looked up to him as a superior. Your lively talents would place you in the greatest danger in an unequal marriage. You could scarcely escape discredit and misery. My child, let me not have the grief of seeing *you* unable to respect your partner in life. You know not what you are about." (378)

A congruity of mind and outlook, and respect for each other that is profound, though never blind, is the basis of the fondness apparent here, as in lesser instances through the novel. Elizabeth's devotion to her father is proof against any criticism that can be levelled at him. The "very strong objections against the lady" which Col. Fitzwilliam had given as the cause of Darcy's detaching Bingley from Jane, Elizabeth knows relate to her family; but she cannot herself admit that anything could justifiably be urged against the father "who, though with some peculiarities, has abilities which Mr. Darcy himself need not disdain, and respectability which he will probably never reach" (187). The only pain she experiences when setting off with Sir William Lucas and Maria to Hunsford, we learn, is "in leaving her father, who would certainly miss her"; and his contentment at her return is evidenced by his more than once during dinner saying "voluntarily to Elizabeth, 'I am glad you are come back, Lizzy'". Is it not therefore inevitable that, when marriage has taken her away from Longbourn, "he missed his second daughter exceedingly", and that he should have "delighted in going to Pemberley, especially when he was least expected"? How could he do otherwise, with a kindred spirit?

\* \* \*

As to her mother, it is a different story. Elizabeth remarkably manages almost throughout, despite the temptations, to maintain filial duty and reserve. But once, and once only, at an apparently idle moment – it is while Mrs. Bennet is tiresomely lamenting the departure of Lydia and her husband – she slips perfectly into Mr. Bennet's ironic mode of inquiry into his wife's cerebral confusions. "This is the consequence you see, Madam, of marrying a daughter", she tells her. "It must make you better satisfied that your other four are single". This mild onslaught upon Mrs. Bennet's chief preoccupation in life evokes a retort that would have gladdened her father's heart.

> "It is no such thing. Lydia does not leave me because she is married; but only because her husband's regiment happens to be so far off. If that had been nearer, she would not have gone so soon." (331)

# iv

# The Enigma of Harriet Smith

Our puzzlement over Harriet Smith begins at the first mention of her. She is introduced as "the natural daughter of somebody", who years before had placed her at Mrs. Goddard's school, where her situation is now that of parlour-boarder. And the action of one of the world's great novels is to turn round the girl pursuing this humble existence: upon her capacity to engage the affections successively of an Elton, a Churchill, a Knightley. The story's credibility and effectiveness, no less, depends on its sustaining the reader's impression that she has qualities which can or will overcome her social deficiency. It takes the shock of Harriet's potential power over Mr. Knightley to awaken Emma to her love for him – and the reality of the distress thus aroused to halt in memorable fashion his proposing to her, in terror lest he should be at the point of confessing an attachment to her protégée. Throughout the novel runs an insistent questioning, whether explicit or unspoken: is Harriet a commendable young woman, a lady in the making – or is she not?

Once she has met her, Emma appears to be certain. She wastes no time, we are told, "in inviting, encouraging and telling her to come very often" to Hartfield (26), resolved to give her the needed sophistication. She has not found her to be clever; but while strength of understanding could not be imparted, Harriet's evident appreciation of what was elegant and witty, her ready embracing of a style of living previously unknown to her, showed that she must have good sense and deserve encouragement. In Emma's first estimation, this was a girl "who only wanted a little more knowledge and elegance to be quite perfect" (23).

The term raises more doubt than it settles. Other than providing herself with an acceptable walking companion, is it Emma's intention to create an agreeable but lesser being, or one who will by these attentions graduate to true estimableness?

An answer is surely present in the fact of what Emma is doing. It is on the face of it unlikely that a woman of her accomplishment would select someone unworthy of her friendship and favour. For Emma is if anything distinguished amongst Jane Austen's heroines by a discernment as to persons in terms both general and particular. Take, for instance, her comment upon Churchill's sudden journeying to London for a haircut, that "silly things do cease to be silly if they are done by sensible people in an impudent way": it is a real insight into human conduct (212). And when, earlier, she has countered Churchill's assertion that no one can be attracted by a reserved character with the retort, "Not till the reserve ceases towards oneself; and then the attraction may be the greater", she is as near as may be to divining the secret of his engagement to Jane Fairfax, which his remark was intended to conceal (203).

Amidst the flow of happenings in Highbury, Emma displays a quick apprehension of motive. She recognises the presence of "great fear, great caution, great resolution" in Jane's determining to stay at her aunt's (285); senses a new happiness after her collecting letters from the post office; and detects her embarrassment at the gift of the piano, and "very reprehensible feelings" as she begins to press the keys (243). The notion that Knightley might be the piano's donor, or that he might care romantically about Jane, are as incisively dismissed as is his own professed indifference to whether he arrives at a dinner party on foot, or in his carriage as properly he should (226, 213). And, despite the force of her initial attraction to Churchill, Emma is soon sure that there can be no building upon "steadiness or constancy" in his disposition, and of her own undoubted preference not amounting to affection for him (265). His engaging manner towards her upon his reappearance in Highbury, further, does not conceal from her a restlessness, "a liveliness that did not satisfy himself", which betokens a lessening of interest in herself – though she is mistaken, and understandably so, in putting it down to a fear of the effect of her personal charms (316).

The same percipient regard plays constantly upon Harriet. It is with an amused, ironic detachment that Emma contemplates "the many vacancies" of her mind (183), and what Sir Thomas Bertram would have described as her "rusticities" of demeanour. Harriet's being nearly recovered from her cold inspires in Emma a wish "that she should have as much time as possible for getting the better of her other complaint", or else "mania", such being her estimate of her young friend's feelings for Mr. Elton. But the emotion as such Emma is far from scorning: she is herself much affected by the artlessness of Harriet's grief when she has disclosed to her the truth of Elton's indifference, and the extent of her own error. But it is not without significance that, in the depth of her conviction at this point "that Harriet was the superior creature of the two – and that to resemble her would be more for her own happiness than all that genius and intelligence could do", Emma can keep her sympathies in check with the wry thought that it was rather too late in the day "to set about being simple-minded and ignorant". The surmise might be held as indication enough that her decision over Harriet will not have been other than clear-sighted (141-2).

\* \* \*

However, there is evidence of a very different order regarding Emma: that while discernment in her is plentiful, her judgment is liable on occasion to impulsive aberration. She shows herself capable of both wilfully suppressing better knowledge, and reversing her opinion without the least awareness of having done so. The matter of the haircut provides an excellent example of the first. Troubled by its air of "foppery and nonsense", she finds Churchill guilty of vanity, extravagance and the like, but also more seriously open to the charge of ungentlemanliness in his disregard of the Westons' feelings, and unconcern as to the impression his behaviour might more generally give rise to. Upon hearing, though, of his highly favourable reception in Highbury, as well as at Randalls, and, from Mr. Weston, how "very beautiful and very charming" he considers her to be, Emma finds that "she must not judge him harshly" (205-6). Nor, when the idea of a ball at Randalls is under discussion, is she able to condemn the lack of gallantry in his studiously ignoring her protest against "a crowd in a little room!" while professing admiration of the phrase. Attributing his persistence to a wish not to lose the pleasure of dancing with her, "she took the compliment, and forgave the rest" (249-50).

Emma's dealings with both the Martins and the Coles are tergiversation itself. The former family, she tells herself at the start, must be coarse and unpolished, quite unworthy of their previous association with her little friend; and as for Mr. Martin when she casts eyes upon him, he "looked as if he did not know what manner was", being, as she proceeds to inform the mortified Harriet, "so very clownish, so totally without air". Her considering, at the end, that "It would be a great pleasure to know Robert Martin", reveals her attitude to have been founded on pure prejudice (475). With the Coles it is much the same, except that they do not have to wait so long for the change to come about. Their invitation to the gentry Emma at first strongly reprehends. Such persons "ought to be taught that it was not for them to arrange the terms on which the superior families would visit them" – though the lesson, she very much fears, will come only from herself. Strangely, however, the prospect of aloofness affords her no contentment, the yielding of her peers demolishes her resistance: and recollection of the dinner party next day is graced with the persuasion that by her presence she must have delighted the Coles – "worthy people – who deserved to be made happy! – And left a name behind her that would not soon die away" (207, 231).

These inconsistencies, while perhaps laudable in denoting the softening of positions that were unduly severe, could scarcely be more evident. They are, it should be noted, in part the outcome of an inability in Emma to tolerate "a subjection of the fancy to the understanding", as Knightley has it (37). In the author's terms, she is "an imaginist": one whose lively mind and unacknowledged feelings can construct "a ground-work of anticipation" for what might prove either fact or fantasy, and cause the last to be treated as substantive (335).

More than this. Engaged as she is in influencing Harriet beneath an appearance of neutrality, Emma is herself subject to a powerful impulsion she can have no idea of, since it arises out of her own disposition. It reveals itself in her besetting imperative of how best to exercise her social superiority. Eminence might be the better word, for Highbury "afforded her no equals", the Woodhouses being first in consequence there. And it is not status alone which makes for self-approval: Emma enjoys full awareness of her claims of personality and intellect. She can boast of having from the start planned the match between Miss Taylor and Mr. Weston, and rejoice at the thought of how "such success has blessed me" (12); and in calmer vein can as hostess demonstrate the "real good-will of a mind delighted with its own ideas" (24), and as a daughter contemplate the benefits of such an affection in her father "as could never find fault" (6).

Might it be that these promptings in Emma combine to evoke instant approval for the girl who upon introduction displays "so proper and becoming a deference" to her, and appears "so pleasantly grateful" for her condescension, and "artlessly impressed" with Hartfield's – and its mistress's – grandeur: whose appreciative response is little less than tribute to all that Emma is, or takes herself to be? For from that moment she is afire with the purpose that is to direct her course through the novel, upon which her every instinct appears to be employed.

> *She* would notice her; she would improve her; she would detach her from her bad acquaintance, and introduce her into good society; she would form her opinions and manners. It would be an interesting, and certainly a very kind undertaking; highly becoming her own situation in life, her leisure, and powers. (23-4)

The aim of Harriet's improvement is to be achieved by the simple means of association with her patroness: mere acceptance is seen as conferring an immediate dignity and worth. It is not therefore surprising that Emma's first remark on hearing of Mr. Martin's proposing to Harriet should be upon his evident determination to "connect himself well if he can" (50); or that she should respond to Knightley's vexation later at the young man's being refused with the deprecatory coolness of, "I cannot admit him to be Harriet's equal". And Knightley's counter-claim thereupon of its being a beneficial offer for Harriet is met with the incensed, "a good match for my intimate friend!" (61-2) This is the outcry of someone as entrenched in the concept of her own superiority as Lady Catherine de Bourgh; and it supports the possibility that Emma's appraisal of Harriet has been unconsciously affected by the idea of her own status and capabilities: that she has viewed her protégée through the distorting glass of her estimate of herself.

In one respect, at least, the above cannot apply: Harriet's remarkable prettiness is beyond dispute. It may be "of a sort which Emma particularly admired" (23), but corroboration is forthcoming from many other observers. There is a certain wonder in Knightley's comment to Mrs. Weston that Emma appears very little concerned with her own handsomeness. She in fact seems more preoccupied with the looks of other women: Jane Austen has endowed her with a distinctive regard for feminine beauty. During her welcoming visit to Jane Fairfax, Emma sits looking at her with the "complacency" which Jane's "very pleasing beauty" inspires. Elegance is its predominant feature; and when afterwards Churchill makes so bold as to belittle it, she is astonished to the point of concluding with some scorn that there must be a very distinct sort of elegance in the fashionable world he belongs to if Jane Fairfax is to be thought "only ordinarily gifted with it" (167, 194).

Emma indeed appears most in accord with Churchill, and as it were mentally attuned to him, when he is itemising Jane's charms to her during their reconciliation at the Westons'. The sentiment of Alexander Pope, that

> Fair tresses man's imperial race ensnare,
> And beauty draws us with a single hair

would have gained her enthusiastic approval. Can it be, therefore, that

Harriet's fine bloom, blue eyes, light hair, regular features and look of "great sweetness" are in effect an assault upon Emma's objectivity, and that "those soft blue eyes" (23-4) are all the while leading her into idealising their possessor for graces not present in her: that, through an excessive preoccupation with what is outward in Harriet, to say nothing of other sources of misapprehension, Emma has come to be quite deluded in her regard for her protégée?

*   *   *

Emma's lifelong acquaintance and future husband certainly thinks so. His view of Harriet, imparted even in the civil tones of his address to Mrs. Weston, is unequivocal. Her companionship will be positively harmful to Emma through the "hourly flattery" that a nature so ignorant will render. She herself will gain only a little polish from the proximity; the "strength of mind" which she sorely needs Emma will be unable to bestow (38-9). This assertion is but a prelude, however, to the scathing assessment Knightley delivers upon discovery of Emma's part in Harriet's declining Martin's proposal. She is a girl of little sense and no information, who is totally lacking in experience, "and, with her little wit, is not very likely ever to have any that can avail her". A prospective lover would face the impediments of "illegitimacy and ignorance"; and Harriet's continued association with Emma will only bring about in her the mischief which "Vanity working on a weak head produces" (61-4).

But this somewhat less than favourable judgment undergoes distinct moderation with the passage of time. Upon Emma's being constrained to confess to him how much Mr. Elton has fallen in her estimation, the gratified Knightley is moved to declare that her friend has greatly risen in his, especially through comparison with the woman Elton has lately taken to wife. He has discerned Harriet to possess "some first rate qualities" which the former Augusta Hawkins is without, amongst them a modest, unassuming nature which makes her "infinitely to be preferred" by any man of sense – who would moreover find, as he has done, that she is "more conversable" than at first appears (331).

True, this is not yet praise of the glowing sort; and some further qualification might be assumed in Knightley's suggestion, in accounting for Harriet's prompt acceptance of Martin upon their meeting in Brunswick Square, that a good-tempered, soft-hearted girl such as she was "not likely to be very, very determined against any young man who told her he loved her" (473). But persuadableness in a young woman, even in a matter of such seriousness, was in that age deemed a virtue, a fact strongly impressed upon the reluctant Catherine Morland and Fanny Price: and had not Knightley himself jestingly taunted Mrs. Weston with it, in respect of the schooling which the young Emma had subjected her to? And on this occasion he is overlooking Harriet's early preference. What though is apparent is that, by the end, his initial disapproval of her has vanished.

No such reversal occurs in Emma's thinking. What she asserts about Harriet during the painful interview subsequent to Martin's being refused is sustained through all that follows; indeed, there is even to be seen in her a heightening of regard for her young charge. Not that she ever comes to imagine Harriet intelligent: but she remains assured that the girl has "better sense" than Knightley is aware of. The same is true of the prettiness and good-nature which he has discounted. These attributes Emma cannot believe to be trivial: the former, she tells him, will hold sway over men until such time as "they do fall in love with well-informed minds instead of handsome faces"; and the latter cannot fail of being a universal recommendation. In her uniting the two, she affirms, Harriet is "exactly what every man delights in": and were he ever to marry, "she is the very woman for you" (63-4).

The last utterance is a riposte, made with jocularity and abandon by an Emma under attack from her formidable opponent. But that it springs from conviction is proved by the manner, later on, in which Harriet's confiding her hopes of Knightley is received. The overpowering sensation in Emma is of course the product of sudden discovery of her own love; but, this set aside – if it may be – her dominant concern at the news is the consequence for himself if he were to marry beneath him: as she pictures it afterwards, "the smiles, the sneers, the merriment it would prompt at his expense". Neither in Harriet herself, nor in the evidence of his fondness she puts forward, does Emma find grounds for dismissing Knightley's attachment as improbable through personal deficiency in its object. The disparity in qualities, as in rank, she is painfully aware of; yet, "Was it a new circumstance for a man of first-rate abilities to be captivated by very inferior powers?" It is very clear that in her own thoughts Emma accords Harriet the full status of a rival: that she sees her in all her attractiveness as little less than the incarnation of her own outlook and philosophy upon womankind (413).

To this conclusion, however, it might be objected that Emma's mind at the time is not capable of any objective assessment. She is in the grip of new and tyrannical emotions: the desire to possess, accompanied by the terror of losing. Love and fear exert their full force; and, were this not enough, she is all the while being afflicted by the bewildering recognition of "The blunders, the blindness of her own head and heart!" The state is one which, in her apprehension, would invest the plainest of plain Janes with the enchantments of a siren (411-2).

When, much later on, assured of the man she loves, and responding to life in the glow of the heart's fulfilment, she expresses to Knightley a wish for the happiness of the betrothed Harriet and Martin, Emma answers his cryptic observation upon the change she has undergone since they last talked on the subject with the self-accusation, "at that time I was a fool". It would be unwise to take the emphatic remark as a confession of disenchantment with Harriet. It is acknowledgement, rather, of Knightley's having been correct in his view of the sphere that life and fortune had marked out for the girl, and of her own lapse in having so romantically departed from the prevailing conventions she is now re-converted to. Here also, therefore, she is not in suitable mood to pronounce upon Harriet's promise. No more, evidently, is Knightley himself, in the indeterminate approval he then voices as to her being "an artless, amiable girl, with very good notions, very seriously good principles, and placing her happiness in the affections and utility of domestic life" (474). If there is apology of a sort in these words, repentance has been present in Emma's little outburst, for the presumption she was guilty of in taking it upon herself to direct another's destiny, and the blunders and embarrassments it has involved them in. The matter of Harriet's personableness – her fitness to attach a man of some consequence, and gain respectability in the world Jane Austen's novels reflect – is left still to be determined.

\* \* \*

The question arises whether Harriet's moderate mental powers would be a hindrance. Emma sees the want of cleverness as adverse; and our own early impressions are of a thoughtlessness and indecision implicit in the "Oh, dear, no" and "Oh! dear, yes!" of Harriet's hasty assents during their first walk (87), the see-saw response to Emma's inference that Mr. Martin does not read – "Oh, yes! – that is, no – I do not know – but I believe he has read a good deal – but not what you would think anything of" (29) – and the agonising at Ford's as to the destination of the purchased muslin and ribbon.

These are minor issues – but not so the cause which brings Harriet with all speed to ask advice upon her receipt of Martin's letter. Emma, we are told, is even half ashamed of her young friend "for seeming so pleased and so doubtful" upon such a theme. The doubt persists throughout their interview, Emma's approval of the letter on perusing it, and inquiry as to whether the answer is to be favourable, gaining little more than a, "well – and – and what shall I do?" and a, "What would you advise me to do? Pray, dear Miss Woodhouse, tell me what I ought to do?" And when, after being with solemn propriety cautioned that marriage is not a proper state to be entered into "with half a heart", and questioned as to Mr. Martin's being "the most agreeable man" she has ever been in company with, Harriet is propelled to a decision, it is couched in terms which reveal it as a lesser triumph of equivocation: "and I have now quite determined, and really almost made up my mind – to refuse Mr. Martin. Do you think I am right?" (50-3)

But indecision at a first proposal is entirely fitting in Harriet's case. She is scarcely out of school,

> a green girl
> Unsifted in such perilous circumstance;

and one, further, whose origins have precluded the ambience and support of a family, as they have acquaintance with the modes of decorum in the imposing world to which she has been so extraordinarily elevated. What is more natural than that Martin's declaration should enhance the sense of her solitariness, and cause her fearfully to seek counsel and comfort from the greatness that has befriended her?

In whatever context she is finally settled, Harriet will not be renowned for resource and positiveness in reasoning. Her capacities as displayed in the novel are limited, from the instance of her wondering whether the solution of Elton's charade is a "trident? or a mermaid? or a shark?" (73) to its being "very odd" that there should be a fortnight and a day's difference between Mr. Martin's birthday and her own (30), or her finding it almost conclusive that Martin's letter of proposal is mere prose, in comparison to the verse of the charade (76). In the latter instances, though, we are encountering the force of affection – as we are in Harriet's tempering the admission of Jane Fairfax's playing being perhaps superior to Emma's with the consoling irrelevance that "if she does play so very well, you know, it is no more than she is obliged to do, because she will have to teach"; or in her designating, and actually enshrining, Elton's bit of plaster and pencil-end as "*Most precious treasures*". Her distaste for Italian singing upon the plea that "There is no understanding a word of it" can, however, admit no such extenuation (232). And if her logic is more admissible when she reacts to Emma's declared resolution never to marry, it derives from the commonplace notions of its being unusual to hear a young woman say such a thing, and "so dreadful" to end up an old maid.

Be this as it may, amidst society at any level Harriet appears a lively and personable presence, taking a keen interest in all its manifestations.

Possessions as such excite her, whether the Martins' "very handsome summer house, large enough to hold a dozen people", or their "two parlours, two very good parlours indeed" – or even the "beautiful goose" Mrs. Martin presents to Mrs. Goddard. But it is people who truly hold her interest. She can, for example, speak with the same "exultation" of Mrs. Martin's having "an upper maid who had lived five-and-twenty years with her" (27-8); and she is most freely herself when concerned with the sayings and doings of others. In the recital of her being discovered by Miss Nash peeping with the two Abbots through the blind at Mr. Elton, and their being scolded away from the window only for Miss Nash to take their place and then good-naturedly call her back to let her see too, and their confiding to each other "how beautiful we thought he looked!" Harriet is at her liveliest (75). She is so again when repeating to Emma, "with great delight", what Miss Nash had told her about Mr. Perry's meeting with Mr. Elton on the road to London, and being informed he is the bearer of "something exceedingly precious" which Mr. Perry inferred must be to do with "a *lady*" (68) – or, for that matter, when she is detailing the comments of anyone upon a subject she has at heart.

Harriet is in fact a social creature. Emma notes her gratitude at being first received in the way she is, and the pleasure she evinces at her hostess's affability and parting handshake; and the responsiveness of a different order when, having been driven to the Martins', Harriet looks around "with a sort of fearful curiosity" before her chilling resumption of relations with them (186). The account of the meeting she gives afterwards so well conveys the naturalness and delicacy of feelings on both sides as to cause Emma alarm. But there was in truth nothing for her to fear. Harriet's protestation earlier, upon realising that Emma must have dropped acquaintance with her had she married Mr. Martin – "It would have killed me never to come to Hartfield any more!" – had expressed what was for her the true scale of values. She feels as strongly as the other the distinction which admission to that demesne has accorded her (54).

This is to be confirmed in intimate terms as Emma endeavours to check her wistful preoccupation with Mr. Elton by mention of the pain which being reminded of her error brings, and Harriet's need for her own sake to acquire the habit of proper self-command. By this hint of thanklessness on her part, Harriet is plunged into a violence of remorse.

> "You, who have been the best friend I ever had in my life – Want gratitude to you! – Nobody is equal to you! I care for nobody as I do for you! Oh, Miss Woodhouse, how ungrateful I have been!" (268)

Nothing becomes Harriet more than this display of "tenderness of heart", as Emma esteems it; nor is the latter wrong in being tempted at this point to consider the young girl as exceeding her in attractiveness. She recognises the want in herself of the capacity for affection which Harriet possesses in having an instinctive liking for people. It is in fact Harriet's social predisposition which puts an end to her tenderness for Mr. Elton. Her sense of the humiliation she is subjected to at the Crown by his ostentatious declining to dance with her is acute: as is her awareness of its dissipation by Knightley's courtly offer of his hand. The whole is an intense experience for her. "Such a change!" she declares afterwards to Emma; "In one moment such a change! From perfect misery to perfect happiness" (342). From what she had said before they quitted the ballroom Emma has realised that it was as if her eyes were suddenly opened to Elton's character; but she does not appreciate the depth of deliverance socially speaking Knightley's intervention has constituted for Harriet: what must be its significance for a nature as open and sensitive as hers.

\*   \*   \*

For she is naturally drawn to the opposite sex; and though always conducting herself with modesty, is not inhibited by undue reserve. There is an appreciative regard for the gentlemen she encounters at

Hartfield, and a respect, which can amount to near-reverence, for their virtues. Mr. Woodhouse's gentleness she had voluntarily remarked on with an esteem verging upon awe; first acquaintance with Mr. Knightley produces the open admiration of his being "so very fine a man!" (32) and aware he would never stoop to her, she can aver that it will remain a pleasure to admire him at a distance, and "think of his superiority to all the rest of the world with the gratitude, wonder, and veneration which are so proper, in me especially" (341).

Is this responsiveness to men the explanation of Harriet's extraordinary amatory career? If it were, it would declare her more than a little of a coquette, and betoken an instability or shallowness of disposition making her unworthy of being taken seriously. If, though, it is not, the question must be asked why in the first place Emma should have found it possible to blight her protégée's early but very real affection for young farmer Martin with little apparent difficulty.

The answer surely lies in the influence which Emma is able so cleverly and determinedly to exert. The slightest suggestion of an attachment from Harriet is enough to call forth the assurance of her being a gentleman's daughter, and consequent necessity of supporting her claim to that status "by every thing within your own power", against those intent upon lowering her, to wit, the Martins. Their meeting with Mr. Martin next day on the Donwell road is prelude to deliberate vilification of his appearance and manner, which brings from Harriet the abashed admission that "he is not so genteel as real gentlemen". There follows a series of denigrating comparisons with men of the Hartfield circle, and introduction thereupon of Mr. Elton's charms, with allusion to the recent "additional softness" of address by which, "If he means anything, it must be to please you". By these means is "the very person fixed on by Emma" now flatteringly introduced to Harriet's shaken sensibilities (30-4).

The business of prevailing upon her to reject Martin's proposal is admirably contrived. There is no urging: instead, an assumption as between ladies of a negative in such a case being without question, of course accompanied by "expressions of gratitude and concern for the pain you are inflicting" – succeeded by affected restrained surprise at the possible existence of "doubt as to the *purport* of your answer". Instantly, the intention is understood. "'You think I ought to refuse him then?' said Harriet, looking down". Ensuing protestations of unwillingness to advise or influence are beside the point: the damage has been done. For her now to accept Martin, as Harriet is acutely aware, would mean the sacrifice of a unique friendship, an abandonment of all that Emma prizes in her and is yet to come to fulfilment, and a betrayal of the social convictions and aspirations that are a true component of her being (51-2).

Such loss and harm, at this early stage of her life, Harriet is not able to contemplate. It is all the more remarkable, therefore, that once decision has been reached and letter despatched, she should display residual independence of mind to the extent of contradicting to her face what Emma has so strenuously impressed on her. Certainly, she concedes, with respect to handsomeness and manner he may not equal others; "However, I do really think Mr. Martin a very amiable young man, and have a great opinion of him" (54). This view, here boldly stated, she can never change, under any form of persuasion, or whatever else may betide: and she confirms it the moment she has the chance.

In recommending Mr. Elton to her, Emma exerts influence of an entirely different kind. The method of disparagement with admixture of pretence, which Martin's inferior social position had made requisite, now gives place to an impulsion of the purest friendship and goodwill. Emma "had no scruple with regard to Mr. Elton", convinced as she is of his being "in the fairest way of falling in love, if not in love already" with her young charge; and while she cannot feel any doubt of having given Harriet's fancy "a proper direction" at the earliest moment by assurance of his admiration, she assiduously follows it up "by agreeable hints". She goes about her task with a delighted certainty, with an enthusiasm at the near-realisation of her dream, by which Harriet, in her inexperience, and fresh from her confined upbringing, is impelled to view matters through her benefactress's eyes (42).

Emma's attributing Elton's attentions to a love for Harriet, gratifying though the idea be, is not a product of her active imagination. She cannot conceive of so inordinate a propensity in him as to have designs upon herself. Her action when he has presented his charade is thus fully expressive of her mind. Smilingly, she pushes the paper towards Harriet with the words, "take it, – it is for you. Take your own". The word *courtship* can be no other than "a very good hint" of the desire to pay his addresses; and the poem's application, as Emma construes it, is so pointed and particular a compliment "that I cannot have a moment's doubt as to Mr. Elton's intentions. You are his object – and you will soon receive the completest proof of it". The purpose it denotes is as clear, she assures Harriet, as her own wishes for her have been since she first knew her (70-3).

The interchange that follows is charged with Emma's exclamations and congratulations: upon the naturalness and desirability of the attachment, its being in every sense prudential and advantageous, its acceptability to friends and family, its elevating tendency, its giving every prospect of happiness through Elton's amiable character, its arising between people called together by situation, and belonging to each other "by every circumstance of your respective homes". The list is all but exhaustive: and the certainty is complete.

As far as Harriet is concerned, Emma speaks with a womanly and social authority that is irresistible; and yet, in the very act of yielding to it, she gives voice to intimations of a contrary sort. "Whatever you say is always right", she cries; "and therefore I suppose, and believe, and hope it must be so; but otherwise I could not have imagined it". The gradations of her acquiescence are significant – as are the reasons she puts forward for her misgiving. Elton in his eligibility is "so much beyond anything I deserve"; his interest in her "is a sort of thing which nobody could have expected"; and she "did not know him, to speak to him, at Michaelmas!" These considerations are commonsense. From their perspective what Emma is urging is most unlikely: but Harriet is without means of resisting it. And soon she is reduced to, "How nicely you talk; I love to hear you. You understand every thing" (74-6).

That she is without defence is the fault, not of herself, but of the usages of social life that directed relations between the sexes.

Attachment and wooing was on both sides a matter of suggestion – delicate, as in the bestowal of compliment, or more explicit, by such gesture or token as the conferring of Harriet's portrait on Elton, or his ceremonious presentation of the charade. By her generous invitations to Hartfield, and the easy sociability she favours him with on Harriet's account, Emma is unwittingly guilty of a liberality that Elton, and even the disinterested Mr. John Knightley, can understand only as encouragement (112). Ordinarily, however, a heedfulness alike in behaviour and in its interpretation is rigorously observed. The Eltons and Knightleys, the Wentworths and Bertrams, agonise over having their discreet inferences "understood" by the beloved: and Harriet is not the least credulous, fanciful or foolish in being guided by Emma's appraisal of the indications in Mr. Elton's conduct. There is for her, in addition, the flattering thought that, just as greatness in Emma's person has lifted her out of obscurity into distinction, so it is now coming more wonderfully to her aid, in Mr. Elton, "who might marry any body!" succumbing to her charms. Could someone as innocent and trusting as she be expected to oppose so felicitous a development, guarded and instructed as she is by an Emma Woodhouse? Harriet is no simpleton in believing herself beloved by this respected gentleman, but reacts to the unusual circumstance as would any well-conducted lady of her tender years.

*     *     *

For Emma, strolling on Hartfield's lawns the morning after the Westons' ball, her head full of gratified musings upon Knightley's gallantry to Harriet, to be confronted with the sight of the sweep gates opening to admit the same Harriet in swooning state on Frank Churchill's arm, after his rescuing her from the gipsies, is a masterpiece of literary construction. No manner of person whatsoever, as Jane Austen mischievously affirms thereupon, would have been dead to the happening's romantic possibilities. Certainly Emma's mind is not proof against them; and afterwards it seems to her the most natural thing in the world that Harriet should be confessing an utter devotion to her champion, though with hopelessness as to the likelihood of a return. Influence, therefore, is not called for here; and Emma, chastened now as she is by recollection of the confusion and distress she had involved Harriet and herself in over Elton, is resolved against the slightest interference, even to the mention of a name. Her advice is therefore what might properly be given to any young woman in this predicament: that matches of such disparity are not altogether without precedent, and that she should observe with the closest attention the beloved's attitude towards her (342).

Harriet is of course talking about Mr. Knightley. The service he had rendered her the previous evening, in its moral and social implication, is for her infinitely greater than the physical deliverance Churchill has just effected. For the latter she is naturally obliged: but by the former she has been captivated. It would have reduced to insignificance any allure that Churchill's forthright conduct might have conferred on him; but in fact Harriet has never even thought of Churchill, except to be conscious of his lacking the distinction, the true gentlemanliness, she had recognised in Knightley. In this she has shown herself possessed of a measure of discrimination which Emma, distracted possibly by romantic schemings, is yet to attain; and at the tense moment when misunderstanding is finally rectified, it is with indignation that Harriet rejects the idea of her having been predisposed as Emma had imagined.

> "Mr. Frank Churchill, indeed! I do not know who would ever look at him in the company of the other. I hope I have a better taste than to think of Mr. Frank Churchill, who is like nobody by his side." (405)

This outspokenness is in part due to the pressure of wounded feelings; but it tends, amid much else, to demonstrate that Harriet is far from being the sentimentalist, the innate romantic, that her dealings might at first suggest.

Falling in love with Mr. Knightley is something she does entirely of her own accord. It is a love born of admiration and esteem; but it arises also from immense gratitude. Knightley's inviting her to dance upon her being scorned by Elton was more than rescue from social affront. It had in truth been a healing in emotional terms, for a nature simple and sincere, shocked and dismayed at sudden perfidy in the man for whom she had entertained a genuine affection. The restoration brought about in her manifested itself outwardly in her bounding "higher than ever" in the dance, and being "in a continual course of smiles": but its effect upon the heart has been far more dramatic, though unseen (328).

It is the greater for what is not present in Harriet's awareness. She has no means of comprehending Elton's ill-treatment to have been a revenge upon Emma for the insult she had administered in specifying his social inferiority, both in the match she had sought to contrive, and that to which he had himself aspired. Quite what sense she might have gained of Knightley's acting to quell a flagrant discourtesy, and in preservation of social decorum, would be hard to determine. But his deepest motive – a wish to remedy the injury to Emma in this public slighting of her friend, an impulse of love itself, which escaped Emma's own recognition – Harriet could not begin to fathom.

As any young woman might, she views what has happened from a personal perspective: sees herself singled out, honoured, redeemed by the man she has throughout identified as in a class apart from the others. His asking for her hand in that situation was the highest compliment that could be paid within the sphere of her experience. With this certainty, enhanced as it is by powerful feelings of thankfulness, she cannot doubt herself as being the woman preferred – and as yet again distinguished by a benign suzerainty seemingly intent on claiming her as its own.

That his inviting her to the dance might be liable to such interpretation would not occur to Knightley. From his social altitude he would, like Emma, never expect persons admitted to a modicum of familiarity to venture above their condition, presuming upon an invulnerability which, however, in the nature of things, a moment's inadvertence might dispel. What preoccupies him is a desire to defend his Emma against affront, and thereby perhaps re-establish himself in her goodwill by graciousness towards a girl he has without doubt judged too severely in the past. The particularity implicit in his so doing can but be regarded, by Harriet and onlookers alike, as a marked attention. The incident, with all that subsequently flows from it in Knightley's seeking with the same determination to cultivate further acquaintance with her, has the appearance in ordinary social terms – as ultimately to Emma's own understanding – of plain romantic attachment.

Harriet is therefore justified in the hopes of Knightley which, in discourse somewhat hesitant and by no means "Methodical, or well arranged" (409), she is later to confide to her sponsor. Bearing in mind the vulnerability with which she is beset by reason of her few years and scant experience, and the pressures social and emotional so arbitrarily brought to bear upon her at Hartfield, her having been or fancied herself in love with him, as with Elton, is in the light of events not at all as remarkable as would appear. And when, freed at last from the affliction of Emma's tutelage, she chances to re-encounter Martin in London, she gives evidence of a praiseworthy maturity, both in the constancy of her first love despite the onslaught made against it, and in the decisiveness she demonstrates in there and then accepting him.

\*　　\*　　\*

When Fanny Price comes to live at Mansfield Park, the Bertram girls are unremitting in their disparagement of their poor cousin for her inferiority. The one respect in which they will allow her any equality with them is disclosed in the grudging admission that "Fanny is good-natured enough". This attribute is largely to be seen in Fanny's compliance with the obligations of her dependent situation at Mansfield, and a readiness to be generally helpful: but with Harriet Smith, it is evident in a variety of relationships in Highbury and at Hartfield. It is perhaps at its most moving in her reception of the news of Emma's having been in error as to Elton's feelings and intentions. There is no blame, no recrimination; instead, a "lowly opinion of herself" which acquits the other of accountability. The affection of such a man, she protests amidst her tears, would have been "too great a distinction". She never could have merited it; indeed, "nobody but so partial and kind a friend as Miss Woodhouse would have thought it possible" (141-2). Both he and the as yet unknown Miss Hawkins are held in high regard: and merely to reflect that he had not thrown himself away is for Harriet "such a comfort!" (272)

Almost as affecting is the sensitivity and tenderness that is demonstrated during her accidental encounter with Mr. Martin and his sister at Ford's, after relationship with them has been abruptly ended. She is near fainting, knowing that she will have turned as white as her gown. In the sister's coming forward and seeming ready to shake hands, Harriet is sorely conscious of the reluctance Elizabeth has contrived to overcome. Her state is not so much embarrassment, as misery at the couple's struggling to hide their pain in complaisance; and Elizabeth's expression of regret at their not meeting now is "almost too kind" for her to bear (179).

But it is surely in her unfailing amiability towards Emma that Harriet's good nature is most apparent. Not only has she repeatedly been led into disappointment and grief, but the friend whose self-centred enthusiasms have been responsible is unmasked at the close as an enemy. Yet so unassuming, gentle and mannerly has she been in all, that not the least semblance of reproach has passed her lips or appeared in her reactions. After she is banished from Hartfield to the John Knightleys in London, Emma can fancy there being present in her letters "something of resentment, a something bordering on it in her style", which, she realises, "might be only her own consciousness" – or in other words, the trick of a merited self-reproach. But even if the former, as she goes on to tell herself, "it seemed as if an angel only could have been quite without resentment under such a stroke" as her appropriation of Knightley. Having, in short, consistently been made a fool of in concerns close to the heart, Harriet reveals, in disposition and in conduct, qualities which by any standard must be seen as admirable (451).

* * *

Amongst them is one which her naiveté and want of cultivation might lead us not to expect. It is to be detected in the conversation with Emma that follows their encountering Mr. Martin. When the mistress of Hartfield, describing him as awkward and abrupt, asks with rhetorical emphasis what he will be at Mr. Weston's time of life, Harriet responds with a solemn, "There is no saying, indeed!"; and the answer of Emma's own providing, that he will have become "a completely gross, vulgar farmer", receives the quiet accord of, "Will he, indeed, that will be very bad" (33). Even allowing for Harriet's inclination and habit of respectfulness, there is, in her demeanour as she meets this slander of the man in whose company she had experienced much pleasure, a deliberative reticence that merits the name of composure.

It is evident also when, under Emma's reproof as to her being "overpowered" by so small a token of admiration as Mr. Elton's charade, she replies with the brevity and self-possession of, "Oh! no – I hope I shall not be ridiculous about it. Do as you please" (77-78). The same tones accompany her appearance before Emma one morning with the Tunbridge-ware box, and confession of having treasured Elton's relics therein. Now professedly an altered creature, she declares a duty and wish to have no reserves from Emma on the subject; and continues, "it is very fit that you should have the satisfaction of knowing it. I do not want to say any more than is necessary – I am too much ashamed of having given way as I have done, and I dare say you understand me". The matter itself is trivial: but the language by which it is conveyed, in its simplicity, has an elegance of its own (337).

More often than not, the mode of address mirrors the mind of the speaker. What, therefore, are we to make of Harriet's words at the moment when realisation has dawned upon Emma that it is Mr. Knightley, and not Frank Churchill, for whom her friend has been nurturing so passionate a regard? "I am sure, but for believing that you entirely approved and meant to encourage me in my attachment", she protests, "I should have considered it at first too great a presumption almost, to dare to think of him". That a degree of sophistication rings through these accents is borne out by the style and content of what ensues. Emma, exclaiming at the "most unfortunate – most deplorable mistake!" she has made, is reduced to a silence. Its significance is not lost upon Harriet, and she responds with an injunction whose mild terms in no way belie its directness. The possibility of such a match has been Emma's own urging: and "if Mr. Knightley should really – if *he* does not mind the disparity, I hope, dear Miss Woodhouse, you will not set yourself against it, and try to put difficulties in the way. But you are too good for that, I am sure" (405-7).

Her meaning could hardly be more plain, yet it is not offensive. Perhaps its very clarity takes any hurtfulness from it: but this can only be when the disposition behind the utterance is innocent and engaging. Of its being so with Harriet, if it were not evident from her previous attitudes, there would be confirmation in her final remark. Until this point, she declares, she had as instructed gone by outward indications of regard in Knightley: "But now I seem to feel that I may deserve him; and that if he does choose me, it will not be any thing so very wonderful". In this speech there is a confidence and womanliness which impresses – and conveys the truth that Harriet has about her at this testing juncture an innate dignity, which others, of more years and greater claim, might well envy (411).

\* \* \*

But does she have the stature which might make some future Austen heroine? The comparison suggests itself with Catherine Morland, who is also at the stage between girl and woman, and certainly not a giant of intellect – but who displays an adherence to principle, a resolution in the face of difficulties, and an ability to think something through which can unsettle even a Henry Tilney. But Catherine has not been subjected to another's authority – save that of Mrs. Allen, which for all practical purposes can be safely discounted. She is obliged almost throughout to stand on her own feet, whereas Harriet, confined to a subordinate role, has small scope for initiative; were she placed in a similar situation, indications are that she would acquit herself creditably. In Fanny Price, by contrast, we observe a profoundly moral nature and contingent strength of personality that can slowly impress itself upon wholly adverse circumstances. But the demands of everyday living oblige her to withdraw into a diffidence which masks her superiority from all who do not know her well; and the hesitation and solemnity of manner which results robs her, in the opinion of many, of heroic pretension.

How different is Harriet's refreshing spontaneity and naturalness. Certainly there is little in her outlook of a detached and speculative kind: her thoughts are a process of responses to events around her, and the hopes, joys and sorrows they give rise to. But the same can largely be said of all Jane Austen's young women: none of them is the stuff philosophers are made of. They are in love with the present as they encounter it, with the men they will marry, when they have found them; and do not seem at the point we know them to be seeking much beyond.

However, there is an exception to what has just been said that concerns Harriet. It has to do with a remark she makes at the end of her account of the distressing meeting with Martin and his sister at Ford's, from which the rain permitted no escape. She would rather have done anything, she tells Emma, than have had it happen: "and yet, you know, there was a sort of satisfaction in seeing him behave so pleasantly and kindly. And Elizabeth, too" (179). In the midst of her anguish at such close contact after the estrangement, she has been struck by the rightness of conduct and delicacy of sentiment in those now permanently distanced from her. Her being so is a piece of wonderment and true reflection. But it is more.

If what defines a gentleman is his predominant desire to set others at their ease, may it not be that a corresponding pleasure in fineness of comportment, and the decencies of social interplay, is what distinguishes a lady? If this be allowed – and who would pronounce otherwise? – it suggests, with much else, that, deceived though Emma may sometimes have been as to character and conduct in the unfolding of events, she made no mistake in her choice of Harriet Smith.

## V

# The Prisoner of Mansfield Park

So great is the impression created in the mind of Edmund Bertram by the festive spirit prevailing in Mansfield Park during his father's absence in Antigua, that he can scarcely conceive of life there ever having been different. Despite the drastic restrictions that marked the latter's return, it takes some moments for Fanny Price's gentle reminders of the unvarying soberness of their former state – the rarity of such a thing as laughter in Sir Thomas Bertram's presence – to register in his awareness. Fanny's own years at Mansfield have rendered her incapable of such illusion. Though not without some measure of happiness, they have been largely a time of oppression for her sensitive being.

A nameless fear created at first by the huge scale of the house, and the magnificence of objects within it, was accompanied by humiliation at the offence noticeably caused to the Bertrams by her uncouthness and lack of manner. It was however the way she was treated by the family that most often mortified her; yet, child as she was, an intuitive sense of its inevitability saved her from despair: "she thought too lowly of her own claims to feel injured by it" (20). She was helped, too, by an obligingness of disposition that made her useful to her betters in running errands and carrying messages: but her celerity in so doing was matched by quickness in comprehending those she served. "She began at least to know their ways, and to catch the best manner of conforming to them" (17).

In this word Jane Austen uses to denote Fanny's response to the surrounding attitudes lies the secret of her development as a person. Throughout much of the novel she can appear merely as a timid, and, for some, insipid conformist: but those who so classify her misread her nature in taking little cognizance of the pressures, domestic and social, to which she is day by day subjected, and of the expedient to which they drive her. She has no choice but submission, if she is to attain to any tolerable mode of living within a context which, for all the comforts it is empowered to offer her, is – from the moment of her being deposited within it till she reaches maturity – inimical to her deepest instincts through its constant reminders of her inferiority and helplessness.

One happening after another shows the completeness of Fanny's subjugation. She performs without murmur the drudge's task of gathering roses in the heat, not daring to give the least hint afterwards of its effect upon her health. Sir Thomas's offering her the coach for the first dinner-party she has ever been invited to causes a degree of astonishment which makes it impossible for her to speak, reducing her to tears of gratitude. His yielding to her unthinking appeal to be allowed to breakfast early with William before his departure moves Fanny to wonder and rejoicing at having carried her point: "she was so totally unused to have her pleasure consulted, or to have any thing take place at all in the way she could desire" (280). And, long after the indulgence of the ball at Mansfield, her habits of compliance make her instantly rise and lead the way to her room, upon Mary Crawford's request for the interview she has anticipated with such loathing.

But it is in the person of Sir Thomas Bertram that her servitude is concentrated. Upon his unheralded reappearance among them, Fanny, though herself innocent of indecorum as they are not, is at the point of fainting; and it is "with desperation" that she at last turns the lock and enters the room. Misgiving at his stern disapprobation is always with her; even her brother William's casual inquiry of him as to whether she is a good dancer produces in Fanny expectation of a cutting reproof, or otherwise a remark of contemptuous unconcern (250). And the heavy step, recognised as her uncle's, and as familiar to her as his voice, outside the East Room consequent upon Henry Crawford's being in the house, provokes again in Fanny the trembling it has often occasioned in the past.

Such, until almost the last, is the condition of Fanny Price at

Mansfield Park. The few spells of respite and relative freedom which she enjoys there originate in a manner which would be amusing if it were not pitiable: when, naturally excluded from the privileges of seasonal socialising, she has been left with the dubious consolation of Lady Bertram's vacuous companionship; and

> the tranquillity of such evenings, her perfect security in such a *tête-à-tête* from any sound of unkindness, was unspeakably welcome to a mind which had seldom known a pause in its alarms and embarrassments. (35)

In their progress to adulthood, Sir Thomas's children go through quite the reverse of Fanny's experience. The buoyancy of youth and consciousness of privilege join to produce in them a kind of delighted ease; the girls especially, handsome, accomplished, and outwardly unassuming, regale in assurance of universal favour. There was however in their upbringing a deficiency whose seriousness had been absent from their thoughts: the lack of affection for a father whose authority had largely determined both its method and content. This truth, which became apparent at the time of his leaving for the voyage to Antigua, is conveyed in a characteristic triple-sentence of Austenian emphasis: "Their father was no object of love to them, he had never seemed the friend of their pleasures, and his absence was unhappily most welcome" (32). Not surprisingly, Fanny shared their relief at his going – but, being herself, is affected nonetheless by her inability to grieve.

It is not until Sir Thomas's homecoming, almost two years later, that his children reach a just appreciation of what his custodianship and dominance at Mansfield has meant for them. Julia's appearing at the door with blanched countenance to announce, "My father is come! He is in the hall at this moment", produces amongst the cast of 'Lovers' Vows' not simply consternation, but "a moment of absolute horror". Uppermost in nearly every mind, certainly in those of his sons and daughters, is the conviction of its being "a stroke the most unwelcome, most ill-timed, most appalling!" (172-5) If, by the right of a disposition prone to disquiet, Fanny's agitation exceeds theirs, they are equal in recognition of that moment's significance. It takes the obvious form of apprehension at what might be the outcome of their error in having indulged in theatricals: but their alarm more truly arises from resumption of Sir Thomas's rule at Mansfield. The fact constrained the children to view past years with new eyes; and what they saw was not only an encroachment upon the blissful freedom of latter months, but a threat to their very existence as persons.

All Maria's hopes had been centred upon her love for Henry Crawford, and expectation that he would declare himself. Disappointment in him brought her to recognise her predicament, and the means of relief afforded by her engagement to the blockish and unloved James Rushworth.

> Independence was more needful than ever; the want of it at Mansfield more sensibly felt. She was less and less able to endure the restraint which her father imposed. The liberty which his absence had given was now become absolutely necessary. She must escape from him and Mansfield as soon as possible, and find consolation in fortune and consequence, bustle and the world, for a wounded spirit. (202)

Ironically enough, it is this decision of Maria's, known to her sister for the desperate remedy it was, which ensures the success of the unlikely Mr. Yates with Julia. She was, we are informed, all but indifferent; what strongly affected her was nothing in herself, but dismay at the tenor life would assume upon Maria's becoming Mrs. Rushworth: "her increased dread of her father and home, on that event". Foreseeing that its consequence to herself would be "greater severity and restraint" caused her without delay to "resolve on avoiding such immediate horrors at all risks", and endowed John Yates with attractions by which he would scarcely have been flattered, had he known them to be the product of his object's "selfish alarm" (466-7).

With the sons it seems otherwise. In different ways they already have considerable independence, Tom being able to draw readily enough on Newmarket's resources at appropriate seasons. He always appears relaxed and confident; yet in both his habitual expansiveness and jocularity might be detected some trace of reaction to the irksomeness he finds in his father's regimen, heir apparent though he be. Amongst the Bertram children as adults, only Edmund is naturally and unaffectedly himself at Mansfield, untroubled by any notion of distancing himself from it – and, let it be said, unawed by its master's bearing.

\* \* \*

What above all makes Sir Thomas formidable is that distinguishing demeanour which social eminence confers on those born to it, or comes mystically to devolve upon the newly-elevated. Though always adapted to the person, it is invariably recognisable as a feature, and indeed a force, in human affairs; and, for an observer of the comedy of life such as Jane Austen, it has an interest bordering upon fascination, as is evident in so many of her characters.

In Lady Russell it is a settled formality allied with seriousness of disposition; in Lady Catherine de Bourgh, a self-regarding imperiousness which treats inferiors and equals alike with audacity. Mr. Darcy has inherited more than a little of his aunt's hauteur. Upon first acquaintance, Mrs. Gardiner finds "something a little stately in him", confined to his air, however, and "not unbecoming" (257); but the author herself is not able to dismiss it so lightly, attributing it (with all the inhabitants of Meryton) to the deeper cause of a nature "haughty, reserved, and fastidious" (16). While Lady Catherine constantly affronts, her nephew contrives as often to offend.

With General Tilney, appearances are almost the opposite. His prevailing mien – the random outbursts of military irascibility apart – is courtesy itself; and, until enlightenment somewhat drastically supervenes, Catherine Morland is set wondering how so charming a man should seem always a check upon his children's spirits. *Persuasion* affords us an example of a potency in Sir Walter Elliot perhaps at once more refined and more sinister. Though in Admiral Croft's opinion and the reader's he appears harmless enough, and not destined to set the Thames on fire, he has the capacity to cast "instant oppression" upon a roomful of vivacious people at the White Hart, reducing them to "cold composure, determined silence, or insipid talk" by his own and his daughter's "heartless elegance" (226), as his creator defines it. All these instances point to manner in itself being the outward token of that transmutation which consciousness of birth, rank, possession and power may work in the human psyche. If the phenomenon can convert the silly and spendthrift baronet of Kellynch Hall into a "formidable" presence in the environs of the Octagon Room (181), it is small wonder that his fellow of Mansfield Park should be the potentate there that he is.

In this regard, Sir Thomas's distance of manner and deliberateness of speech are ominous. His grave looks cause fearfulness in the child Fanny from the moment of her arrival, rendering vain his well-intended condescensions. The accompanying slowness of utterance is also unpropitious, but has its amusing aspect, as Jane Austen is well content to demonstrate through the agency of his spouse. Lady Bertram will long since have come to terms with it, by habitude or sheer oblivion; but when, at the Grant's, Sir Thomas twice inquires into her enjoyment and success at the game of Speculation, "no pause was long enough for the time his measured manner needed" (240). And not entirely void of humour is his perplexity at Tom's sick-bed, where he "knew not how to bring down his conversation or his voice to the level of irritation and feebleness" (429).

Like the Duke of Wellington after him, the baronet has no small-talk, nor either the capability of indulging it: as Mary Crawford sagely remarks on hearing of the brevity of Edmund's letter to his father, "Who could write chat to Sir Thomas" (288). And Edmund is himself concerned at the impression his father might in their few encounters have made upon the same Mary: "his reserve", he confides to Fanny, "may be a little repulsive" (119). This is no idle supposition. That Edmund's sisters, for all their erudition, were deficient in generous and modest aptitudes, is the result precisely of the barrier of estrangement existing between them and the supervisor of their instruction. Sir Thomas had been unaware of what was wanting in the girls,

> because, though a truly anxious father, he was not outwardly affectionate, and the reserve of his manner repressed all the flow of their spirits before him. (19)

The same can be said respecting highly personable guests who are vouchsafed welcome at Mansfield Park. The Honourable John Yates, despite his financial adequacy being suspect, positively abounds with self-confidence. Acutely frustrated at the demise of 'Lovers' Vows', and at the irrationality responsible for it, he is strongly disposed on the way back from Mansfield Wood to argue his host into some sense; but when they are sitting round the same table, he begins uncomfortably to distinguish a something in Sir Thomas which makes him "think it wiser to let him pursue his own way, and feel the folly of it without opposition" (191). Similarly, while the whole party, including Henry Crawford and William Price, is entertained to dinner at the Grants', Mary Crawford in her turn has endured the destruction of her hopes by Sir Thomas's insistence that evening upon Edmund's being Thornton Lacey's resident clergyman. She sits considering him with decided ill-will – and suffering the more from not daring to ridicule his position by one of her witty diatribes, through "that involuntary forbearance which his character and manner commanded" (248). If it could still the promptings and enforce the compliance of such free-born sophisticates as these, what chance was there of a Fanny Price prevailing?

Although Sir Thomas's ascendancy arose out of intrinsic merits, it was enhanced by the strength of principle: the concept of what is befitting, in all circumstances, in relation to a person of his degree. It can be summed up in words like pride, and decorum. It is pride of family that makes him solicitous for the advancement of the Price sons in their careers, and evokes the "unanswerable dignity" with which Mrs. Norris is rebuffed when she opposes the carriage being ordered for Fanny: " – My niece walk to a dinner engagement at this time of the year!" (221) These gestures of his are laudable enough; but they should be understood in the light of the specific condition attached to Fanny's being brought to live under that roof at the beginning. She was always to be kept from the illusion, never be allowed to lapse into the gratification, of imagining herself a Miss Bertram. The imperative of rank was to be obeyed, the "distinction proper to be made between the girls as they grow up" (10) inflexibly enforced, the claimless newcomer kept in her place through all her formative years.

Exactly the same resolve directs Edmund's conduct at the prospect of Charles Maddox being invited to play the role of Anhalt in 'Lover's Vows' which he has himself declined. According to Tom, Maddox is as gentlemanly a man as is to be seen anywhere, and Edmund knows no harm of him: but the problem lies not in his endowments, but in his birth. For he is not a Mr. Bertram; and his admission into the intimacy of a family group, and, indeed, the familiarity which acting must promote, would constitute such a betrayal of aristocratic obligation, so great a sin against the dues of precedence, as only the word evil can convey. Hence Edmund's decision to take the part after all, despite the shame of inconsistency, and the testimony of his own conscience (153-6).

There must ever be something admirable in devotion to principle, for it both requires, and confers, fortitude. But it may also exact penalties, through the dulling of sympathies and vision it can effect. The necessity of wealth in persons of social eminence is for Sir Thomas an absolute. Thus it comes about that, though he is struck with puzzlement at Mrs. Norris's refusal to do anything for Fanny, after having been so urgent for her adoption, the germ of discernment so born is quelled by his sister-in-law's assurance that the whole of her possessions is destined for his family. His far stronger impression of Mr. Rushworth's being an inferior young man is for long held in check by the gratification he had felt, on news of the engagement reaching him when abroad, that this was "a connexion exactly of the right sort; in the same county, and the same interest", an alliance "unquestionably advantageous" (40). Upon coming to realise later that, far from loving Rushworth,

Maria did not even like him, he is ready to act for her and release her; but, though unpersuaded by his daughter's assurance of esteem for her betrothed, he will not urge the ending of "an alliance which he could not have relinquished without pain". Instead, he reasons with himself that Rushworth might yet improve; that Maria's declared confidence of happiness should be believed; that a woman not marrying for love would be the more likely to find solace and enjoyments amongst her family; and so on. His own profound satisfaction at the prospect of a connexion "which would bring him such an addition of respectability and influence" makes him, in Jane Austen's observation, "very happy to think any thing of his daughter's disposition that was most favourable for the purpose" (201).

Sir Thomas's perceptions and judgment concerning persons, even in respect of a daughter, have been blinded and distorted by social dogma – as they had, by implication, in the limitations he had decreed for the growing Fanny Price. For many years he regards her, not as she is, but in terms of the situation these preconceptions have assigned her. Whatever of kindness there might be in his invitation, on the last morning before his departure, for William to visit Mansfield when his squadron comes home, it is dissipated by his coldly imparting to her his fear that "he must find his sister at sixteen in some respects too much like his sister at ten" (33). Fanny is timid and shy still; but her uncle speaks largely in ignorance, as Edmund was in a position to have informed him. It is not insignificant that what first brings her truly to his notice is the being struck on his return by "her equal improvement in health and beauty" (178): in other words, by her looks – to which considerations of social standing do not apply.

\*   \*   \*

Unlike Sir William Lucas in his contentment at Lucas Lodge, the baronet has more to do than think with pleasure of his own importance. As an ancestral landowner he takes very seriously his traditional duties, not only to tenants, but to the nation at large, by supporting its institutions and the upholding of its moral standards. His readiness to pursue without compromise the latter obligation is clearly to be seen in the doom of 'Lovers' Vows'. Not content with proscribing the theatricals and dismantling the theatre, his determination impels him to "wipe away every outward memento" of a play noted for its indelicacy by consigning to the flames, with the ardour of a zealot, every unbound copy that meets his eye (191).

No less emphatic is the response he makes to Henry Crawford's polite expression of a wish for tenancy at the Thornton Lacey parsonage. In declaring pleasure at the prospect of Crawford's becoming a neighbour in any house but this, and affirming the naturalness of the young man's not having thought much on the subject, Sir Thomas's rejoinder is equally polite, even excessively so. But in his assertion that he would be "deeply mortified" if Edmund were to become an absentee parson, and the insistence that only a resident clergyman can know a parish's needs, there lies a severity which cannot be mistaken – and, in the remark that ensues, finality itself. Edmund will be aware "that if he does not live among his parishioners and prove himself by constant attention their well-wisher and friend, he does very little either for their good or his own."

By this "little harangue", as the author names it, Crawford is reduced to silence, and successive bows; and in the gathered company activity is likewise thwarted for its duration. The sentiment is impeccable: but its statement and mode of delivery, coming as it does in the midst of after-dinner talk, is at least unfortunate. The party is being treated to somewhat of a lecture; and – if such comparison dare be made – there is in its ponderousness more than a slight similarity (absurdity apart) to the address on the duties of the rector of a parish with which Mr. Collins favours guests at the Netherfield ball (PP247-8).

The position taken regarding Maria's adultery with Crawford is still more rigid, yet by the standards of that day, admissible. Sir Thomas will not offer "so great an insult to the neighbourhood" as to allow her to appear at Mansfield Park: so to do would be "affording his sanction to vice" (465). The same estimate and purpose at first moves Mr.

Bennet with regard to Lydia; but the having attained the status of matrimony enables the manner of her securing a husband to be seen as an *étourderie*, so justifying her reception at Longbourn.

There is no doubting the correctness, and uprightness, of Sir Thomas's promptings and actions in these respects. They are morally founded, and abundantly well-meant: but they are enforced with a stringency which tends all but to nullify their essential worth. That the style of their imparting is involuntary, and the effect almost certainly uncomprehended, should however always be borne in mind in relation to the person from whom it emanates. This is what Fanny Price may well have been trying to tell herself when, at the sounds denoting Sir Thomas's approach, "The terror of his former visits to that room seemed all renewed, and she felt as if he were going to examine her again in French and English".

Nothing in the novel is more indicative of the extent to which Fanny is in subjection than the treatment she receives from her uncle upon his coming to tell her of Henry Crawford's application for her hand. What will be the outcome of the message he bears is for him certain, and he derives happiness from the conviction that in giving it, "he must be gratifying her far more than himself". His astonishment on hearing his niece's exclamation that it is out of her power to return Mr. Crawford's good opinion is such that he is reduced to echoing her words – as he does again, with Lear-like disbelief, after asking directly whether it is Fanny's intention to refuse the offer of marriage.

What he had seen of relations between the two convinced him of the contrary. Her cool, seemingly unaffected reception of his advances had by the accepted standards been entirely proper. From it he was confident that she had given her lover "as much encouragement to proceed as a well-judging young woman could permit herself to give": where her deportment was concerned he has "no accusation to make". Beyond this observation he is initially aware of nothing that could or should have led her to an adverse decision. The reason his questioning extorts from her – "I – I cannot like him, Sir, well enough to marry him" – moves Sir Thomas to comment "in a voice of calm displeasure" on its strangeness: of there being "something in this which my comprehension does not reach".

He sets out thereupon conscientiously to understand, with searching inquiries on the state of her affections, and – watching her intently – her estimate of his son Edmund's tenderness toward Mary Crawford. Satisfied in these respects, he is left only with the question whether she has cause "to think ill of Mr. Crawford's temper?" The possibility of there being objections of a more serious kind is beyond his calculation; and Fanny is inhibited by loyalty and fear from referring to Crawford's unprincipled conduct with Maria and Julia.

As the interrogation has proceeded, and Fanny's unaccountableness become more pronounced, so her uncle's displeasure is more evident; and at its end, in a tone of "cold sternness", he impresses upon her the grounds of its being so. The conduct which, he asserts, has "disappointed every expectation I had formed", is simply an incompliance with the conventions and norms of society for a young woman of any pretension. Fanny has, in effect, shown an independence of spirit "which in young women is offensive and disgusting beyond all common offence" – the unpersuadableness incompatible with womanliness itself – in respect of deference to the wishes and wisdom of her elders, and thought for the social elevation an advantageous match would bring her family. But she is more culpable still in the requirement of love, which has apparently brought this obduracy about: her not feeling for Crawford "what a young, heated fancy imagines to be necessary for happiness". For this inordinate longing has impelled her to the ultimate failing in a female: the sin against wealth, property and station, the intolerable affront to the expectations of the whole social order. Had either of his daughters, Sir Thomas declares, at the tirade's logical conclusion, declined a proposal with only half the eligibility of Crawford's, he "should have thought it a gross violation of duty and respect". – This, however, does not end it. His final utterance is of another nature, and left incomplete.

> "You do not owe me the duty of a child. But, Fanny, if your heart can acquit you of *ingratitude* –" (312-9)

It is understandable, especially in terms of the reigning conventions, that Sir Thomas should regard Fanny's refusal as a defiance of his overriding will as master of Mansfield, so identifying himself with the demands of the system that has made him what he is. But the sudden change of tone, the new note, amidst reproof, of urgency and tenderness, is striking. It may be attributed to a final and calculated invoking of known susceptibilities, rather than be thought evidence of an unguessed-at sensitivity in the speaker. To think that the baronet might have seen himself as another Lear, protesting to a lesser Regan, "I gave you all –", only to receive the chilling answer, "And in good time you gave it", would be to picture him as more deserving of sympathy at this point than his sobbing, afflicted niece.

In the same way, were we not, like the astonished Fanny earlier, to ascribe to the momentary workings of time and distance the change of manner in her uncle upon his unannounced return from Antigua – the unexampled kindness, the voice "quick from the agitation of joy" (178), the dissipation of former severity by a new-found affectionateness – we should incur the notion of Sir Thomas being a quite different person from him whose harshness was soon to reduce to misery the girl who declined to take his approved Henry Crawford for husband.

*   *   *

The crisis point of the novel is not the painful interview between them in the East Room, despite appearances, but a slighting comment upon Fanny which Mrs. Norris makes to her brother-in-law immediately afterwards, when, at his suggestion, the girl had taken to walking in the shrubbery to regain her calm. There are, she tells him, faults in Fanny which she has often observed:

> "she likes to go her own way to work; she does not like to be dictated to; she takes her own independent walk whenever she can; she certainly has a little spirit of secrecy, and independence,

and nonsense, about her, which I would advise her to get the better of."

Sir Thomas's reaction comprehends more than the walking in question. It is that as a general reflection on Fanny, "nothing could be more unjust, though he had been so lately expressing the same sentiments himself"; and he tries repeatedly, as well he might, to turn the conversation, but without any success until half through dinner (323-4). At an earlier stage, he would certainly have disapproved of Mrs. Norris's acquiescence in Maria and Julia's scorn for Fanny's lack of learning; and he would doubtless have deemed ill-advised her inculcating in the girls' minds the doctrine that it was unnecessary for their cousin to be as accomplished as they, and "much more desirable that there should be a difference" (19). But Fanny's being constantly at her relations' beck and call, the exclusion from their social round and pretensions – the life in fact of subservience – has been entirely in accord with Sir Thomas's expectations for her, and, be it said, with Fanny's own. If he had then been present, he would have shared the startlement of the hearers, and the indignation of some, at his sister-in-law's accusation, when Fanny declines the others' united wish for her to act in 'Lovers' Vows', that she was showing herself "very ungrateful indeed, considering who and what she is" (147). But had it not been his requirement throughout that "who and what she is" should always be impressed upon her: that the "dependence of her situation", as Jane Austen puts it, ought as was proper to be part of her everyday consciousness? (150)

Nor can it be denied that the same spirit and logic in her aunt Norris which would grudge Fanny a horse of her own, or set her cutting and carrying roses in the sun, or evoke wrath upon her being offered the carriage, is at work in the deploring the Grants' lavish meals – "And round their enormous great wide table too, which fills up the room so dreadfully!" – as in the denying little Dick Jackson the casual hospitality of the servants' hall. After pausing for breath, preparatory to urging Fanny not to be putting herself forward during the dinner visit, she gives unambiguous voice to the doctrine in the ample phrase, "The nonsense and folly of people's stepping out of their rank and trying to appear above themselves" (220-1).

With the affirmation *per se*, Sir Thomas is perfectly in agreement. But it is a very different spirit within him which soon thereafter is asking Fanny what time she wishes the carriage to come round for her, and crushing so disdainfully her aunt's objection. As decisive is his remark, when she is swift to assure William of the impossibility of there being a dance at Mansfield when Julia and "dearest Mrs. Rushworth" are not present, that "the absence of some is not to debar the others of amusement". It requires some minutes' silence for the lady's vexed surprise to abate (252-3).

The surprise in Sir Thomas exceeds this when he comes into Fanny's room to find no fire burning in the grate on a day when snow is on the ground. His repetitions of, "here must be some mistake", and, "Here is some great misapprehension which must be rectified", and the shortness of sentence in, "You are not strong. You are chilly. Your aunt cannot be aware of this", are indications of a mind momentarily shocked. Customary utterance is resumed in the address which follows in defence of what he now comprehends to have been Mrs. Norris's prohibition. Influenced perhaps by her own hardiness, she has been a constant advocate, "and very judiciously", of young people's being brought up without undue leniency. The principle is good in itself, but had in Fanny's case been carried rather too far. It has not escaped his notice that, in the worthy attempt to prepare Fanny for the "mediocrity of condition" which appeared to be her lot, there was "sometimes, in some points, a misplaced distinction". Professed confidence that she will harbour no resentment does not hinder him from urging his niece never to fail in treating her aunt Norris "with the respect and attention that are due to her" (312-3).

The pointedness of this homily, its meticulous excusing of his sister-in-law, and cautioning Fanny against ill-will, shows the degree of Sir Thomas's own reprehension of her conduct, in truth his dismay at her measures. For Mrs. Norris has been made the representation of the precepts, customs and values, in their negative aspect, which motivate him: by Jane Austen's art, she is the embodiment of his own social persona. Herself of no status, fortuitously raised to the dignity she now exults in, she imposes upon her hapless niece the aristocratic code, without the compensating graciousness by which at its best aristocracy is always accompanied. And in the process of so doing she has been revealing gradually to her brother-in-law the realities of the system that operates around and within him: significances which nurture, habit and elements of character have combined to withhold from his ordinary consciousness. She is in effect the glass in which, as life proceeds, he finds himself mirrored.

Hence the gathering annoyance, amounting to detestation, which he comes to feel respecting her. His opinion of her, we are told, has been sinking from the day of his return from Antigua.

> He had felt her an hourly evil, which was so much the worse, as there seemed no chance of its ceasing but with life; she seemed a part of himself, that must be borne for ever.

The sentiment appertains to the tragic. It is one which makes memorable appearance in the impassioned King Lear, when he addresses his daughter Goneril as, "my flesh, my blood, my daughter; / Or rather, a disease that's in my flesh, / Which I must needs call mine" (II. iv. 224-6). Strictly, Mrs. Norris is not Sir Thomas's flesh and blood: here are not matters of regality and statehood, or even of life and death, but of mere domestic disquietude. But when subsequent events procure the banishment of his sister-in-law from Mansfield Park, the relief is "so great a felicity" to its master that, but for the bitterness of memories connected with her departure, he might almost have been tempted "to approve the evil which produced such a good" (465-6). The presence of feelings like these suggests that, as with Lear himself, so with Sir Thomas Bertram: typical of them as their attitudes and policies of rule, national or domestic may be, they are in neither case expressive of the underlying self.

Nevertheless, the baronet has been guilty of deliberately propelling Fanny Price into a known evil, in compliance with those same principles which, as put into practice by Mrs. Norris, were becoming, seemingly, ever more displeasing to him. The scheme he devises, to his unsuspecting niece's delight, for her to spend some months in Portsmouth, "had very little to do with the propriety of her seeing her parents again, and nothing at all to do with any idea of making her happy". His wish was that she should be "heartily sick of home before her visit ended"; that, brought into "a sober state" through deprivation of Mansfield's luxuries, she should form a "juster estimate" of the establishment at Everingham which Henry Crawford was offering her; that, in short, his purpose of disposing her fitly in marriage by Mansfield's concepts should be achieved.

The shortcomings, even vices, of an order of society, and of those upholding it, ought not to be allowed to obscure its virtues from us. This, Jane Austen profoundly believed; and the latter part of the thought we may be sure was present to Sir Thomas in his "experiment" (369). A preponderant system's injustices and wrongs having been exposed to the reader in their effect upon Fanny, and particularly in the person of Mrs. Norris, so the Prices' household and its inhabitants are made to bring painfully into view the consequences of incompliance and exclusion. Miss Frances Ward had married to disoblige her family, in the common phrase, and incurred a debilitating penalty. For, as Fanny is grieved to discover, in that context of deprivation life itself is crudified, and the values even of kinship can be brought almost to nothing.

It is less the smallness of rooms and thinness of walls that is disconcerting on her arrival than the house's being "the abode of noise, disorder, and impropriety" (388): a bewildering impression of nobody in the right place, and nothing being done as it ought to be. Her father, upon encounter, was in his uncouthness and vulgarity a figure of repugnance; having observed that she was grown and would be wanting a husband soon, he "seemed very much inclined to forget her again" (380). That the mother, bearing a faded likeness to her sister at Mansfield, was "a dawdle, a slattern", incapable of any kind of domestic management, was harrowing enough; but more wounding to Fanny was her seeking in vain for the appearance in Mrs. Price of a will to know her better, or inclination for her company: absence of the benison of affection itself (390). And the neighbourhood and its people came to afford much the same demoralising apprehension: "The men appeared to her all coarse, the women all pert, every body underbred" (395). Such was the impact upon a privileged upbringing of poverty's endless attrition.

Eagerly did Fanny recall the peace, elegance and tranquillity of Mansfield Park, as they were brought to her remembrance by their very opposites; and with fondness did she now reflect upon a habitation where each person's importance was recognised, and everyone's feelings consulted: where, "If tenderness could ever be supposed wanting, good sense and good breeding supplied its place" (392). Her present abode was, however, not entirely without such propensities: to her surprise Fanny discovers their existence in the "proper opinions of what ought to be" (397), and "an innate taste for the genteel and well-appointed" (419) in her sister Susan, and wonders at this evidence of natural light of the mind amidst such an environment. But it was her just conviction nonetheless that, outside the pale of social privilege, those finer sensibilities which gladden human interrelationship are endangered, if in the end they are not entirely overcome.

The truth of her belonging now is inescapably upon her. Mansfield is her home. Delicacy towards her parents causes her not to betray it in speech, but to talk of returning to Mansfield, or going back into Northamptonshire – until longing defeats caution, and the word home interposes itself. She knows to the full the implication of this change. It means that the house, the style, the system, which had for long years tyrannised over her, is now claiming her as its own: that (to employ the idiom of Mammon to the fallen angels in their infernal dwelling) Fanny's former tortures have become the very elements of her being: that her uncle's stratagem to engender within her proof of her conditioning has beyond measure succeeded. That Sir Thomas has finally triumphed, and his niece's durance is complete.

\* \* \*

The novel's ending does allow itself to be construed in these terms, but only figuratively so. To apply them in any realistic sense would be to belie the nature of both principals concerned. Time's mutations have affected all at Mansfield Park; and Fanny Price by now is an attractive and cultivated person. Edmund's friendship and Lady Bertram's dependence have established her position there; the Bertram girls' departure accords her the distinction of social recognition and invitation, of Mary Crawford's favour, and of Henry's proposal; and the Crawfords' disgrace opens the way to her heart's desire. What once was discomfiture and suffering in her uncle's house has been subtly transformed into an influence of fulfilment and delight.

As for Sir Thomas, though from his dominance he must appear the spokesman and stern administrator of social rigidities, he has given indication through events of certain characteristics more than a little at variance with what is to be expected – and we have tended to assume – of the occupant of such an office. When considered in their light, the flow of spirits and geniality upon his return to Mansfield, and the fervency of his plea to Fanny respecting ingratitude, are revealed to be, not exceptions, mere tricks of an otherwise austere mind, but rather evidence of a benignity, which a patrician aloofness normally conceals. And it will remain hidden, unless – as with Fanny Price herself – the possibility exists in the reader of coming to terms with a forbidding manner.

In all his dealings Sir Thomas manifests an apparently innate concern and respect for persons. Perhaps the gift of a substantial living to his friend Norris had betokened it; but certainly the ten year-old Fanny is its object while still in her parents' home at Portsmouth. Mrs. Norris's eager proposal that they should undertake the care of the Prices' eldest daughter inclines Sir Thomas to debate and hesitate for more than one reason. Unless what they did for her was entirely adequate, "there would be cruelty instead of kindness in taking her from her parents"; if she were unable, later on, to marry greatly, they must consider themselves engaged to secure to her "the provision of a gentlewoman". But what causes him most apprehension is the matter of the distinction of rank upon Fanny's adoption. That it must be maintained is unquestioned: but his mind is not so much exercised on its preservation, as upon the need for it to be humanely applied, so that there would not be "the smallest degree of arrogance" in his daughters towards their poor relation, and that the latter's inequality should be made clear to her "without depressing her spirits too far". What above all would be called for in her upbringing, he insists, is "delicacy" (6-11).

In specifying this quality, Sir Thomas is not demanding of others something not present within himself. How else could it come about that his stricture upon Tom for his extravagance, which has forced the sale of the valuable living intended for his brother, should amount to no more than the moral reproof of, "I blush for you, Tom" – albeit delivered "in his most dignified manner"? At this point his composure is perfect. It is less so when, upon opening the door of the billiard room, he finds himself on a theatrical stage, and confronted by a ranting young man "who appeared likely to knock him down backwards". Though angered by being affronted in his own house and finding himself part of "a ridiculous exhibition", he is yet able to receive so undesirable a stranger "with all the appearance of cordiality which was due to his own character" (182-3). The demands of baronetal dignity are here incumbent; but in dealings with his offending children and sister-in-law a similar forbearance and gentleness is evident. With the former there is no remonstrance: the sweeping away of their preparations is to be sufficient rebuke. And the hint at lack of sound judgment that he cannot help giving Mrs. Norris at her sanctioning the play is evaded by that lady's instant eloquence on other subjects.

Even his ruthlessness over 'Lovers' Vows', which appears unseemly and dictatorial to present tastes, has sufficient justification in the intellectual climate of the age. The conjunction of fear of Jacobinism and influence of the evangelical revival had made condemnable any example of lavish frivolity or dissipation in the residences of the privileged. The inclinations of Sir Thomas's own temperament are naturally involved; but his action might suggest a responsiveness to the contemporary mood of moral earnestness by which his children, with Edmund's exception, were seemingly unaffected.

In other respects the baronet is admittedly the embodiment of fixed and established notions, no more so than in his preparedness to allow Maria's marriage to go forward upon the prospect of his own advantage, financial and political. But the explicitness of his daughter's assurances ought not to be ignored; nor should the "solemn kindness" with which she had been addressed, and the undertakings made for her release "if she felt herself unhappy in the prospect of it" (200). Though the consent Sir Thomas gives in the end is mistaken, it cannot be attributed to the lack of paternal affection: at the wedding, Jane Austen tells us, he felt as an anxious father must feel, and was "indeed experiencing much of the agitation that his wife had been apprehensive of for herself" (203).

Emotions of this nature are neither exceptional nor remarkable in a man whose thoughts centre upon his children's interests and welfare to the extent Sir Thomas's prove themselves to do. In seeking to ascertain whether Fanny has a liking for either of his sons, he puts to her his judgment from observation that Tom as yet has no thought of marrying, but that Edmund "has seen the woman he could love" (317). Concern for his younger son never lessens. Amidst his "poignant" suffering over the mischance that so suddenly befalls Maria and Julia, he is by perception and conjecture also sentient of what must be Edmund's pain, in the loss to him of Mary Crawford through her brother's turpitude. It is he who, realising how much it must have been increased by the pair's late interview, and anxious on that account "to get him out of town", orders that Edmund should take Fanny back to her aunt, "with a view to his relief and benefit, no less than theirs" (452-3).

The positive gratification he derives from the society and advancement of the young is shown in his treatment of William Price. No sooner had the joyful Fanny received the letter sent into Portsmouth when his ship is at anchor, than her uncle is "most collectedly dictating" a kind invitation in reply. He and his younger son have separately connived to ensure that the meeting of brother and sister should have no witnesses; and with "sympathetic alacrity" the two of them frustrate Mrs. Norris's intended "rushing out into the hall as soon as the noises of the arrival reached them". It is with complacency that Sir Thomas surveys the delight William and Fanny have in each other's company, which every day renews; and, in calling upon his nephew to recount his exploits, his chief object is not their interest in themselves, but "to understand the recitor, to know the young man by his histories"; and he derives great satisfaction from their evidence of his excellent abilities, from "every thing that could deserve or promise well" (232-6).

The same pleasure is conferred by consideration of the growing personableness of William's sister. When the news of Fanny's unprecedented invitation to dinner had been imparted by a troubled Lady Bertram, his reaction, after a short deliberation, was, "Nothing can be more natural" (218). Though his own agreeing, later, to dine with the Grants proceeds from simple good-breeding, it is not unconnected with his having noted, "in a grand and careless way that Mr. Crawford was somewhat distinguishing his niece" (238). The fact has bearing upon his decision "to gratify so amiable a feeling" as William's wish to see Fanny dance – and, as Jane Austen comments, "to gratify any body else who might wish to see Fanny dance" (252). She is, for him, "an interesting object" at the ball. Her informing him that Crawford is to be her partner for the first dance is "exactly what he had intended to hear" (272-5); and it is concern for her exhaustion that decrees, first, that there must be no more dancing, and, thereafter, that she go immediately to bed. A reason for the last, the author implies, is that he might mean to recommend her as a wife to Crawford – who else? – "by shewing her persuadableness" (281).

Such has been Sir Thomas's regard for his niece, before the denunciation he inflicts on her for rejecting Crawford. Its vehemence has arisen out of concern that is real, if based on devout conviction of the rightness of all he has been urging. Appreciation, as it comes, of what the distraught girl has been enduring, with the self-accusation implicit in his inward acknowledgement of her being "very timid, and exceedingly nervous", brings about however a complete change of attitude, which the writer amusedly chooses to describe as, "a little relenting". The idea dawns upon Sir Thomas of an approach quite other than that of blame: that a little time, a little pressing, a little patience, and a little impatience – "a judicious mixture of all on the lover's side" – might work their usual charm on a mind so affected. Not only is Fanny spared the immediate interview he had proposed, and left in quietness for a spell; but her uncle upon return brings comfort in word and manner, speaking only to urge self-control, and to advise her with kindness "to go out, the air will do you good" (320-2).

When they are together some while afterwards, Sir Thomas, having decided against further importunity, contents himself with informing her of his meeting with Crawford, and congratulating her on having inspired "an attachment of no common character" in the suitor's perseverance – something which her being as yet little acquainted with love's "transient, varying, unsteady nature" might have led her to undervalue (330). Agreeably, if belatedly, she is advised that he has no intention to persuade her into marriage against her will; and, having before determined the family should have no knowledge of what had taken place between them, he declares the subject to be closed. Few would disallow that his altered conduct, towards a niece blameable in his eyes, is deserving of words like restraint, considerateness, and courtesy.

Whether these same terms can be applied to his immediately thereupon sending Fanny to Portsmouth is another matter. But it is done in pursuance of her interests as he views them. Henry Crawford's firmness had impressed him; and, wishing this wealthy aspirant to be a model of constancy, he fancies the best means of ensuring that end will be by not trying him too long. From Edmunds's report – he will no longer trust his own judgment – he finds his hope that Fanny would miss Crawford once he were gone has been dashed; and the plan he contrives for her temporary separation from the elegances she had grown used to is "a medicinal project upon his niece's understanding", to inculcate such moderation of outlook as would make her a wiser and happier woman all her life (369). From social imperative, and ignorance of the character of its owner, he had equated Everingham with her happiness. He was on both counts mistaken: and yet he had not erred. After so hurtful an experience of uprooting, the sampling of underprivilege was what Fanny needed for the attaining of selfhood.

In her case, Sir Thomas's wisdom justifies itself; but in other respects more nearly affecting him, and of disastrous consequence, it is soon revealed to have been flawed. The family of which he is head is plunged in sorrow by the untoward events at the close; each person and life undergoes alteration – but none to the extent Sir Thomas does himself. Horror at the scandalous break-up of Maria's marriage, with Julia's attendant elopement, and dismay at the destruction thereby of his hopes for three of his children, overthrows his confidence in the engrained assumptions that have throughout governed him. And, of all the family, he is the longest to suffer, from consciousness of having been mainly responsible for the calamity which had befallen them. It is with anguish "never to be entirely done away" that he now contemplates having brought up his daughters in a manner that deprived him of acquaintance with their natures, and hindered in them apprehension of what is most laudable in conduct. While their aunt's indulgence had implanted assurance in them, his own severity had prevented their confidences: and it had been to the superficialities of knowledge and deportment, not the disposition itself, that he had given attention. The instruction in religious precept they received had been theoretical only: they were "never required to bring it into daily practice" (463). As with the training of the youthful heir of Pemberley, in fact, they had been "taught what was *right*", but not to correct their disposition; given good principles, "but left to follow them in pride and conceit" (PP369).

Scarcely could Sir Thomas comprehend how so material a fault had been possible; but, bitterly as he now deplored it, there had been an error of still greater magnitude, now all too readily understood. His cognizance of Maria's feelings towards her intended husband should have made him prohibit their union: in allowing it, "he had sacrificed the right to the expedient, and been governed by motives of selfishness and worldly wisdom" (461): by those considerations of affluence and station which so far had been sacrosanct.

Enlightenment had been dearly bought. Now that it was come, however, his one great object must be "to bind by the strongest securities all that remained to him of domestic felicity". In his desolation he has noticed the developing friendship between Edmund and Fanny, and pondered upon the more than possibility of their finding in one other consolation for the disappointment each had undergone. His consent when applied for is given joyfully, by a man now "Sick of ambitious and mercenary connexions", aware of the meretriciousness of rank and wealth in comparison with "the sterling good of principle and temper". It is with eagerness that he has promoted this match between his son and the girl he recognises to be the daughter he wanted. Though his former notions and harshness of bearing had deprived him of her early love, it had been "an error of judgment only"; and their mutual attachment, we are informed, now became very strong (471-2).

Through all her childhood dread of him, Fanny had come to recognise her uncle's fine qualities; and, even at the height of distress of his causing, can esteem, in him, a man "so discerning, so honourable, so good" (318). Yet almost to the very last he is presented to us as a distant, formal figure lacking in appeal and warmth – as if the concept of degree with which he is identified has chilled and repressed the humanity within him. By displaying in a personality whose motives are entirely admirable the severities of his infliction, the warping of his nature from which they had issued, and the ultimate renunciation of his former standards and very being, Jane Austen is engaged in nothing less than implicit censure of the social order beneath which she lives: of the inhumanities and injustices, smaller and greater, which, with all its excellences, it correspondingly nurtures. And, upon the baronet's alliance in kith and in soul with a penniless commoner of his own fostering, the confining bars are sundered, the grim walls dissolve, and the prisoner of Mansfield Park steps forth, self-liberated, from a life-long captivity.

# Notes

1. Milton, *Lycidas*, 1.87
2. *Much Ado About Nothing*, IV. ii. 85-92
3. I.ii.31
4. IV.vi.110-11
5. III.iii.416-7
6. *Johnson on Shakespeare*, ed. W. Raleigh, London, O.U.P., 1957, p. 196
7. I.vii.39-41
8. T. B. Macaulay, 'The Diaries and Letters of Mme D'Arblay', *Edinburgh Review* (January 1843) lxxvi, 561-2; cited by B. C. Southam, *Jane Austen: The Critical Heritage*, London, Routledge & Kegan Paul, 1968, p. 122
9. Letter 142, to James Edward Austen, 9 July 1816, *Letters* ed. D. Le Faye, O.U. P., 1996, p.316
10. II.iii.248-9
11. *Jane Austen*, The Novelists Series, 2nd edn, London, Arthur Barker, 1966, p. 50
12. I.iii.211-12
13. *Measure for Measure*, I. iv. 34
14. op. cit., pp. 67, 73
15. *The Merchant of Venice*, II. ix. 32-3
16. I.iv.35
17. op. cit., pp. 74-5
18. ibid., p. 88
19. *Jane Austen: A Biography*, 1938, revised edn, Indigo, 1996, p. 161
20. ibid., p. 162
21. *Knightes Tale*, l. 1761
22. op. cit., p. 88
23. II.ii.52
24. op. cit., p. 82
25. *The Two Gentlemen of Verona*, V. iv. 110-12

26 *An Ideal Husband*, First Act, Mrs. Cheveley to Sir Robert Chiltern.
27 Letter 155, 23 March 1817, *Letters*, ed. D. Le. Faye, p. 335
28 *Jane Austen: A Biography*, p.293
29 op. cit., p.296
30 op. cit., p.137
31 I.ii.158
32 D. Le Faye, op. cit. p.333